Main Speak: Quotes from the Work of Sinclair Lewis

Michael Fridgen

Publisher's Note: This is a book of excerpts with commentary. The commentary is original material of the author, Michael Fridgen. The excerpts are from the various novels of Sinclair Lewis. The excerpts belong to the novels of which they were originally published and are used here according to the fair use policy of copyrighted material.

ISBN 13: 978-0-9968574-5-1

Dreamlly Books: **Minneapolis, MN**

Table of Contents

Michael Fridgen

Introduction

"There is to be seen a glorious 20-mile circle of some 50 lakes scattered among fields and pastures, like sequins fallen on an old paisley shawl."

-Sinclair Lewis on Inspiration Peak, Minnesota

This quote is found on a historical marker atop Inspiration Peak in the Leaf Hills Moraines of Minnesota. Don't feel too inspired by the name of this pinnacle; it rises only four hundred feet over the prairie. Yet, in this part of Minnesota it towers above everything else. My grandparents lived nearby in Urbank. My sisters and I would look for any excuse to get away from their farm—Inspiration Peak was always a good diversion. If Sinclair Lewis were to write about my grandparents, I imagine the text would look something like this: *Fridgen's paternal grandparents were not grandparents in any usual sense of the title. This was mostly due to the fact that they had never been even grand parents.*

Happy to be away, we'd climb up the surprisingly steep path through the dense trees. We could never visit in the winter when huge drifts of snow blocked all approaches to the area. But the bird sounds of spring and the colors of the fall made up for the mosquitoes of summer. Eventually, we'd reach the small clearing on the top of the kame (a geologic dome created by a glacier). At that place there is only a small bench, the historical plaque, and lots of peace. The view is incredible as the prairie stretches in all directions. Several lakes really do shimmer as if they were Lewis's metaphorical sequins. The lucky pilgrim will have the chance to see a thunderstorm rolling miles away.

Main Speak: Quotes from the Work of Sinclair Lewis

I had no idea who Sinclair Lewis was as I read the historical marker countless times throughout my childhood. There was no mention that he was the first American to win the Nobel Prize for Literature. I didn't know that his most recognized novel, *Main Street*, was so sensational for its time that it outsold the Bible. Had I known that I would eventually grow up to become obsessed with the man, I'd have paid more attention and read some of his books. But then, Sinclair Lewis is not for the young and naïve. He was a realist; he did not write for the romantic, even though romance is a pivotal aspect of much of his work.

Growing up in Minnesota, I was forced to read who all Minnesotan English teachers consider the most brilliant writer from our state: F. Scott Fitzgerald. But Fitzgerald's world was as foreign to me as China or Argentina. Nothing of his work spoke to me or taught me anything about the reality of life. One teacher, to whom I was brave enough to disclose my disdain for Fitzgerald, suggested that I read the work of Garrison Keillor, a more rural homegrown author. Keillor's arrogant style, masked by nostalgia, did little to inspire me. I didn't discover anything about myself in either Gatsby or Wobegon.

Ironically, it was the summer after I left English teachers behind by graduating from college, that my literary world exploded. It was 1993. My sister was marching in the Alexandria, Minnesota Vikingland Parade. Just twenty-six miles from where Sinclair Lewis was born, I sat along the street-curb on a faded lawn chair. An organization of some sort was raising funds across the road by selling used books. Escaping the boredom of waiting for the parade, I went to look through the books. There, I saw a copy of *Main Street* for twenty-five cents. I recognized the author from my childhood plaque at the top of Inspiration Peak.

It was the best twenty-five cents I've ever spent (and that includes the time that Cold Spring Bakery was selling donuts at four for a dollar). From the first page, I was enthralled with the plight of Carol Kennicott and her struggle with the village virus of Gopher Prairie. This, finally, was a part of Minnesota literature I could relate to. This was the Minnesota I knew. Carol's world was not black and white–it was full of grays, purples, and even one brilliant rainbow. I knew Carol because I saw her inside myself. Most importantly, I saw sides of Carol that I didn't like, and I hated having to admit that those negative aspects were also a part of me.

As I read through the vast work of Sinclair Lewis, I found many more complicated personalities that I both loved and hated. I'm proud to claim that the wonder and enthusiasm of Bethel Merriday is part of who I am. I love that Aaron Gadd's skepticism is alive and well in my mind. And when I look in the mirror and see Doremus Jessup, I wink at him and hope he never leaves me.

But I also know that, sadly, Elmer Gantry lives in my soul. His self-righteous proselytizing comes out from time to time– much to my dismay and enjoyment. That sad sack Babbitt is inside me, too, as is the workaholic Martin Arrowsmith. The novels of Sinclair Lewis are not for the insecure. His realistic style haunts the reader with questions about themselves that they will try to ignore for weeks. (Am I being too hard on Babbitt? Is he not as sad a sack as I proclaim? Oh, damn you Sinclair Lewis...couldn't you make your protagonists easier to protagonize?)

Sinclair Lewis was born Harry Sinclair Lewis in Sauk Centre, Minnesota on February 7, 1885. He spent all his childhood and teenage years in tiny Sauk Centre with his physician father. He went to Yale and then tried to find himself all over the country before realizing that he was nowhere to be found. Of course, it's no surprise to me that Sinclair Lewis could not find himself among the literary thinkers of the early 20th Century. He needed to create his own genre, and that is exactly what he did.

He struggled with a few mediocre novels. Then, in 1920, Carol Kennicott stepped off the train and onto *Main Street*. Sinclair's life, and the future of American Literature, would never be the same. He followed the phenomenal success of *Main Street* with a long string of bestselling novels. He was awarded the Nobel Prize for Literature in 1930–the first American to win the award.

Unfortunately, Sinclair Lewis faced the decline of his creative powers by self-medicating with alcohol. After the destruction of two marriages and one liver, he died on January 10, 1951. He's buried in a small cemetery on the edge of Sauk Centre. Once each year I place flowers on his grave–he'd probably hate my homage and chastise me for wasting time on the dead when there are so many wonderful words waiting to be strung together. (Note: For a most comprehensive biography of Sinclair Lewis, read Richard Lingeman's excellent book *Sinclair Lewis: Rebel from Main Street*.)

I continue to be enthralled by his writing. Just as some people can watch the same movie multiple times and enjoy it each time, I'm still amazed by the insight of *Dodsworth*, even though I've read it over and over again. Coincidentally, I married a man with the last name of Lewis–I often joke that the only reason I married him is because of his last name. (Sometimes, I go so far as to state that I'm not even gay–I just married a person of my same gender because he had the right last name!) Fortunately for me, and much more fortunately for him, my husband has also developed a love for the novels of Sinclair Lewis.

People have asked me, "If Sinclair Lewis was so brilliant, why isn't he more widely read?" I always have a blunt answer, because my opinion is quite definite: We don't like to read Sinclair Lewis because he knows too much about our private lives and it makes us uncomfortable.

There is nothing introspective about F. Scott Fitzgerald. All I've learned from him is that silly rich people are–well–silly rich people. Reading Fitzgerald is like going to the zoo. I look at all the animals and see how different they are, but I don't ponder too much about what it's like to be a Pygmy Hippo because I know I'll never be a Pygmy Hippo. Sinclair Lewis, however, doesn't allow me to look at life like I'm at the zoo. While reading Lewis, I am compelled to ask: Is it alright to agree with something the most bigoted man on Main Street just said? Why am I still attracted to Elmer Gantry even though he just stabbed his friend directly in the back? Am I a Pygmy Hippo? The water in my Pygmy Hippo cage used to be clear, but now it's murky–is the zookeeper a wonderful person or not? Is it my own Pygmy Hippo fault? Or, is that just the way of it?

To read Sinclair Lewis is to read about that dirty side of ourselves that we don't want to acknowledge. It makes us confrontational, uncomfortable, and feels just plain disgusting. This is why Sinclair Lewis is not more widely admired. He was too good at his job.

I'll conclude this introduction by telling the rest of the story from the historical marker at Inspiration Point. The plaque goes on to state that Sinclair Lewis was dismayed that Minnesotans did not know their own "haunts of beauty". So upset was he, the marker states, that Lewis intended to write to the governor of Minnesota, "asking His Excellency if he has ever stood on Inspiration Peak".

It's my hope that you will find humor, wisdom, and a bit of yourself within these quotes from the brilliant writer of Stearns County, Minnesota.

Qualities Common to All Works of Sinclair Lewis

In order to gain an introduction into who Sinclair Lewis was as a writer, I've compiled a list of items that are found in all his work. When a particular theme or style finds its way into twenty-two novels, it's safe to assume that it was an intriguing part of the author's personality.

- The most attractive physical quality in a woman is good-looking ankles. I can't think of even one instance where Lewis writes about breasts, but ankles are mentioned hundreds of times. I'm not sure what, exactly, constitutes a good-looking pair of ankles, as it's assumed that the reader just knows this. It must have been a phenomenon unique to Lewis's time. A good set of ankles will turn heads everywhere from Gopher Prairie to Berlin.
- Cocoanut Cake is absolutely delicious and should be served at any type of function. I don't believe there are any novels of Lewis's that do not mention cocoanut cake at least once. (Yes, this is how Lewis spelled cocoanut during his lifetime.)
- Run-on sentences are perfectly fine when used as a literary device to provoke a sense of exasperation and exhaustion in the reader. Some "experts" believe that Lewis's use of run-on sentences make his writing somehow inferior. They are mistaken. Lewis asks a lot from his readers and he knows that we are intrinsically lazy. If he can't rely on us to think our way into feeling frustrated, then he will certainly force us into frustration through the clever use of this most misunderstood literary device.
- Just like in real life, characters come and go often in a Lewis novel. Don't be surprised if a character believed to be the

protagonist disappears in the fourth Chapter as the real star emerges. It's also common for a major character to appear in the last ten percent of the book.

- Do not discount nameless characters. Often, Sinclair Lewis will use an unnamed source to make the most astounding observation of a novel's theme. These sources take the form of doormen, fellow train passengers, store clerks, and passers-by on the street. I suppose this also occurs in real life, except that we never get to know what strangers are really thinking about us. The insight of the author portrayed through minor characters is often brilliant.

- Closure is not a luxury afforded to readers of realism. While it seems modern culture teaches that all situations deserve closure, that concept is not realistic. There are not many completely happy endings in the work of Sinclair Lewis. There are endings that are downright sad. There are endings that are not even endings. Just as in real life, this is the way it is.

- Prohibition. Since Prohibition was the major cultural shift of the time, it features prominently in most of Lewis's work. (For those readers around the globe, Prohibition was a period when the United States banned all sale and consumption of alcohol.) We can most definitely tell from his writing that Lewis believed Prohibition was a phenomenal failure. There was no shortage of liquor during Prohibition and often the policy made life complicated and downright dangerous.

- Lewis was infatuated with transportation and hotels. He lived at a time when travel first became possible and relatively efficient. Born in the age of trains and boarding houses, he lived to see jumbo jets and modern luxury hotels. Travel is a theme in most of his books, and several are completely centered around the topic.

- Due to the era in which his books were written, language involving the identity of minority populations is different than what we use today. The mistreatment of women and people of color are major themes in many of Lewis's novels. Today, readers may question his choice of terminology, however, Lewis uses the words that were available to him at the time. There is a lot more on this topic that I will discuss as I present each book.

Michael Fridgen

About this Book of Quotes

Compiling the selections for this book was a difficult task, indeed. I love so much of Sinclair Lewis's work that I was tempted to include entire Chapters. But it would have been impossible to carry around such a book.

I mainly chose quotes that are profound or humorous—or both. Lewis had a habit of using the English language in a unique way, and I've included many of these selections as well.

I discovered more quotable sections from the novels he wrote while at the peak of his craft than I did from his early and late works. In this book I've listed the novels in chronological order; however, feel free to read them in a different order. Lewis's most brilliant period of writing occurs from 1920's *Main Street* through 1935's *It Can't Happen Here*.

Lewis was a prolific writer. For the scope of this book, I have limited myself to the twenty-two works that were published as complete novels. Sinclair Lewis wrote many short stories for various magazines. Mostly, he wrote these during periods in his life when he needed money. Consequently, these short stories were often written for a particular audience, and usually don't provide too much insight into the mind of the author. I've not included any of these short works here. I have, however, included novels that were originally serialized in magazines and later published as whole books, because Lewis had a voice in their editing.

A word about spoilers: It is my intent that the reader will enjoy these quotes so much that they will seek to read the original novels. Consequently, I've attempted to avoid dramatic spoilers as much as possible. With that said, it may be possible to gain a vague understanding of where a story is heading by reading through the quotes. Some readers may be annoyed by this and should consider themselves warned.

Selections that were taken from the narrative of a novel are listed here without quotation marks. When I include a selection of text that was taken from words that a character spoke or thought, I've used quotation marks. I have also attributed these types of quotes to the character that owns them. Please keep in mind that authors frequently have characters say things to let us know about the character's personality–something a character says is not representative, or even indicative of, something that Sinclair Lewis may have thought himself. I often see the words of Elmer Gantry featured in quotes that are attributed to Sinclair Lewis. This isn't fair as Lewis made Gantry say many things that the author would most certainly not agree with.

I will be most pleased if readers find their own quotes from the work of Sinclair Lewis that I have not listed here. I will also aggressively defend my choice to include a quote that the reader believes should have been disregarded.

And now, without further ado, let's begin our literary journey through one of America's greatest minds.

Michael Fridgen

Our Mr. Wrenn: The Romantic Adventures of a Gentle Man (1914)

There are seeds of the future Sinclair Lewis in *Our Mr. Wrenn*, but they don't sprout or even germinate in his first novel. Here, Lewis honed his craft as a writer that cherishes realism. His brilliant satire does not exist in this book—he did not win the Nobel Prize for *Our Mr. Wrenn*.

With all that said, Mr. Wrenn, as a character, is developed and described beautifully. Mr. Wrenn is a lonely soul desperately weary of being alone. Sinclair Lewis retreats to this character often in his work. Unlike most modern authors, we get to know a lot about the inner mind of Sinclair Lewis by reading his books.

It's also important to note that romance features heavily in *Our Mr. Wrenn;* it's even mentioned in the title. When professors of literature think about Sinclair Lewis, they think about the prize-winning satirist. However, Lewis is truly a romantic. Or, at least, he very much wants to be romantic. It is a legitimate statement that every Sinclair Lewis novel is a romance, even the unhappy ones.

Since *Our Mr. Wrenn* was a debut novel, it's fitting to talk about another first-time novelist. Sinclair Lewis had two sons. (Lewis was twice divorced and had a child with each wife.) His eldest son, Wells, wished to follow in his father's footsteps and become a writer. Reportedly, Sinclair was thrilled with this prospect and he assisted Wells with his first book, *They Still Say No*. Wells, like his father, dwelt as a writer of realism.

They Still Say No is far superior to *Our Mr. Wrenn*. But to be fair, Sinclair Lewis did not have the advantage of having a Nobel Prize-winning father helping him to write—Wells Lewis did. Soon after publication of his first novel, Wells enlisted into World War Two. He hoped the experience of being in the military would offer fantastic stories for future writing. Wells did well as an officer and served throughout the entire war in Europe. Unfortunately, in 1944, just before the war ended, Wells was killed by a sniper. The world will never know the amazing literature that might have been.

Don't read *Our Mr. Wrenn* for the story. Read it because it exists. Or better yet, read it after *Main Street, Babbitt,* and *Elmer Gantry*–seeds are much more impressive after having seen an oak tree.

[A word about Sinclair Lewis and language relating to minority populations: It's important to remember that writers in 1914 encountered a different world than do the writers of today. Sometimes, Lewis's characters say disparaging things about certain groups of people. Sinclair Lewis does this to let the reader know how truly ignorant those characters are. An ignorant character may use the n-word to describe Black people; unfortunately, that was quite common in 1914. These types of characters also use 'mollycoddle' to describe gay men–mollycoddle was the 'faggot' of the early 20th Century. As a realist writer, Lewis does not sugar-coat language in the way we might today. Antagonistic characters may also display anti-Semitism and overt sexism. Again, do not make the assumption that Lewis himself held such views. On the contrary, he makes his ignorant characters say these horrible things to let us know how despised they should be.]

CHAPTER 1

Mrs. Zapp was a fat landlady. When she sat down there was a straight line from her chin to her knees. She was usually sitting down.

CHAPTER 1

As he wavered home, drunk with weariness, his fear of losing the job was almost equal to his desire to resign from the job.

CHAPTER 3

Mr. Wrenn appreciated England's need of roast beef, but he timidly desired not to be gored by steers, which seemed imminent, before breakfast coffee.

CHAPTER 5

Mr. Wrenn: "I've been learning something on this trip. I've always wanted to just do one thing—see foreign places. Well, I want to do that just as much as ever. But there's something that's a whole lot more important. Somehow, I ain't ever had many friends."

CHAPTER 6

Of that loneliness one could make many books; how it sat down with him; how he crouched in his chair, be-spelled by it, till he violently rose and fled, with loneliness for companion in his flight. He was lonely. He sighed that he was "lonely as fits." Lonely—the word obsessed him. Doubtless he was a bit mad, as are all the isolated men who sit in distant lands longing for the voices of friendship.

CHAPTER 7

A day of furtive darts out from his room to do London, which glumly declined to be done. He went back to the Zoological Gardens and made friends with a tiger which, though it presumably came from an English colony, was the friendliest thing he had seen for a week. It did yawn, but it let him talk to it for a long while.

CHAPTER 9

He suddenly threw his chin back, high and firm, in defiance. He didn't care if he was wicked, he declared. He wanted to shout to Istra across all the city: Let us be great lovers! Let us be mad! Let us stride over the hilltops. Though that was not at all the way he phrased it. Then he bumped into a knot of people standing on the walk, and came down from the hilltops in one swoop.

CHAPTER 13

He thought almost every night about making friends, which he intended—just as much as ever—to do as soon as Sometime arrived.

CHAPTER 17

On Nelly's lack of reaction at the news that Mr. Wrenn was meeting another woman: So lacking in jealousy was Nelly that Mr. Wrenn was disappointed, though he didn't know why. It always hurts to have one's thunderous tragedies turn out realistic dialogues.

Michael Fridgen

The Trail of the Hawk: A Comedy of the Seriousness of Life (1915)

During his second attempt at a novel, Sinclair Lewis continues to find his voice. However, sometimes in order to discover their true spirit, a writer will experiment with multiple styles. Here, Lewis's experimentation wanders further away from his future voice. Consequently, *The Trail of the Hawk* feels less like Sinclair Lewis than does *Our Mr. Wrenn*.

The Trail of the Hawk is the story of Carl Ericson and is told in three parts. Part one describes Carl's upbringing in the small Minnesota town of Joralemon. He has a few triumphs and failures while navigating through high school and college. Carl then harshly joins the real world and struggles through a number of jobs. Eventually, he finds a passion for mechanics which leads to a life as an early aviator.

Part two, by far the best section of the book, details Carl "Hawk" Ericson's life as a famous aviator. Today, we take airplanes for granted. It's difficult to completely grasp how amazing it was for people of 1911 to see an airplane. It's also difficult to understand why anyone would want to be a pilot when the death rate was so incredibly high. Carl rises to the challenge. Obviously, a lot of research went into the writing of this novel. Sinclair Lewis had no knowledge of aviation because *nobody* had any knowledge of aviation. To see a human being fly though the air must have seemed like pure magic–Lewis captures this spirit quite well in part two.

Part three describes Carl's attempt to fall in love. This part seems to drag on a bit and, mostly, I wish Carl would just get to it. But the end of the novel reveals that there was a great purpose for all this meandering.

Main Speak: Quotes from the Work of Sinclair Lewis

The only section of *The Trail of the Hawk* that I read over and over again is part two. As an aviation enthusiast myself, I love learning about that romantic and perilous time when flying was rare. The excitement of flight persuaded people to wait for hours in a field just for a brief chance to see a plane. The perilousness of it all was much more dangerous than us modern people can know. I often think of Carl Ericson when I board a plane bound for my beloved Minneapolis/St. Paul International.

And, even though this isn't the most stellar of Lewis's works, it contains one of my favorite sentences of all literature. The last line of the book, uttered by Carl Ericson, has become sort of a motto for my life. I've recorded it below as the last quote from *The Trail of the Hawk*.

CHAPTER 1
He loitered outside the shed, sniffing at the smoke from burning leaves—the scent of autumn and migration and wanderlust.

CHAPTER 2
Bone Stillman: "Don't forget this, son: nothing outside of you can ever hurt you. It can chew up your toes, but it can't reach you. Nobody but you can hurt you."

CHAPTER 3
Ben Rusk on automobiles: "My mother says she don't believe the Lord ever intended us to ride without horses, or what did He give us horses for? And the things always get stuck in the mud and you have to walk home—mother was reading that in a newspaper, just the other day."

CHAPTER 5
Bone Stillman on hearing that Carl wants to study Law: "Look here. Don't you know you've got a chance of seeing the world? You're one of the lucky people that can have a touch of the wanderlust with-

out being made useless by it–as I have. You may, you may wander in thought as well as on freight-trains, and discover something for the world. Whereas a lawyer–They're priests. They decide what's holy and punish you if you don't guess right. They set up codes that it takes lawyers to interpret, and so they perpetuate themselves. I don't mean to say you're extraordinary in having a chance to wander. Don't get the big-head over it. You're a pretty average young American. There's plenty of the same kind. Only, mostly they get tied up to something before they see what a big world there is to hike in, and I want to keep you from that. I'm not roasting lawyers–Yes, I am, too. They live in calf-bound books. Son, son, for God's sake live in life."

CHAPTER 5
Bone Stillman: "You want to know that there's something ahead that's bigger and more beautiful than anything you've ever seen, and never stop till–well, till you can't follow the road any more. And anything or anybody that doesn't pack any surprises–get that?–surprises for you, is dead, and you want to slough it like a snake does its skin. You want to keep on remembering that Chicago's beyond Joralemon, and Paris beyond Chicago, and beyond Paris–well, maybe there's some big peak of the Himalayas."

CHAPTER 5
On Mrs. Cowles and her attempt to get rid of Carl Ericson: Mrs. Cowles shivered. No one could possibly have looked more like a person closing a door without actually closing one.

CHAPTER 7
On Carl's first attempt with a glider: The wind lifted the plane again. With a shock Carl knew that his feet had left the ground. He was actually flying! He kicked wildly in air. All his body strained to get balance in the air, to control itself, to keep from falling, of which he now felt the world-old instinctive horror.

CHAPTER 8
Professor Frazer: "And, most of all, a general realization that the fact that we cannot accomplish all these things at once does not in-

dicate that they are hopeless; an understanding that one of the wonders of the future is the fact that we shall always, in all ages, have improvements to look forward to."

CHAPTER 9

Carl Ericson, as he defends Professor Frazer: "You apologize or I'll punch your face off," said Carl. "I don't understand Professor Frazer's principles like I ought to. I'm not fighting for them. Prob'ly would if I knew enough. But I don't like your face. It's too long. It's like a horse's face. It's an insult to Frazer to have a horse-faced guy listen to him. You apologize for having a horse face, see?"

CHAPTER 12

The Minneapolis train pulled out, with Carl trying to appear commonplace. None of the sleepy passengers saw that the Golden Fleece was draped about him or that under his arm he bore the harp of Ulysses. He was merely a young man taking a train at a way-station.

CHAPTER 15

He slept in a narrow bunk near a man with consumption. The room reeked of disinfectants and charity.

CHAPTER 17

His first impression of an aeroplane in the air had nothing to do with birds or dragon-flies or the miracle of it, because he was completely absorbed in an impression of Carl Ericson, which he expressed after this wise: "I—am—going—to—be—an—aviator!"

CHAPTER 18

It is a grievous heresy that aviation is most romantic when the aviator is portrayed as a young god of noble rank and a collar high and spotless, carelessly driving a transatlantic machine of perfect efficiency. The real romance is that a perfectly ordinary young man, the sort of young man who cleans your car at the garage, a prosaically real young man wearing overalls faded to a thin blue, splitting his infinitives, and frequently having for idol a bouncing ingénue, should, in a rickety structure of wood and percale, be able to soar miles in the air and fulfil the dream of all the creeping ages.

CHAPTER 23

Carl "Hawk" Ericson: "Carmeau killed yesterday, flying at San Antone. Motor backfire, machine caught fire, burned him to death in the air. He was the best teacher I could have had, patient and wise. I can't write about him. And I can't get this insane question out of my mind: Was his beard burned? I remember just how it looked, and think of that when all the time I ought to remember how clever and darn decent he was. Carmeau will never show me new stunts again."

CHAPTER 25

Carl did not know much about opera. In other words, being a normal young American who had been water-proofed with college culture, he knew absolutely nothing about it.

CHAPTER 26

On Carl Ericson rebuking a guest at a party: That was the only time Carl was not bored at the party. And even then he had spiritual indigestion from having been rude.

CHAPTER 28

Carl Ericson on high art: "I think it would be a good stunt to get along without any art at all for a generation, and see what we miss. We probably need dance music, but I doubt if we need opera. Funny how the world always praises its opera-singers so much and pays 'em so well and then starves its shoemakers, and yet it needs good shoes so much more than it needs opera—or war or fiction. I'd like to see all the shoemakers get together and refuse to make any more shoes till people promised to write reviews about them, like all these book-reviews."

CHAPTER 30

Carl Ericson: "Most of my life I've been working with men with dirty finger-nails, and the only difference between them and the men with clean nails is a nail-cleaner, and that costs just ten cents at the corner drug-store."

CHAPTER 34

The tyranny of nine to five is stronger, more insistent, in every department of life, than the most officious oligarchy. Inspectors can be bribed, judges softened, and recruiting sergeants evaded, but only the grace of God will turn 3.30 into 5.30.

CHAPTER 36

Aunt Emma Truegate Winslow was the general-commanding in whatsoever group she was placed by Providence (with which she had strong influence). At a White House reception she would pleasantly but firmly have sent the President about his business, and have taken his place in the receiving line.

CHAPTER 38

On Ruth Winslow and her relationship with Carl Ericson: She still insisted that she was not in love with him; hooted at the idea of being engaged. She might some day go off and get married to some one, but engaged? Never! She finally agreed that they were engaged to be engaged to be engaged.

CHAPTER 40

She taught Carl to say "dahg" instead of "dawg" for "dog"; "wawta" instead of "wotter" for "water." Whether she was more correct in her pronunciation or not does not matter; New York said "dahg," and it amused him just then to be very Eastern.

CHAPTER 40

Carl Ericson: "I wonder if it isn't pure egotism that makes a person believe that the religion he is born to is the best? My country, my religion, my wife, my business—we think that whatever is ours is necessarily sacred, or, in other words, that we are gods—and then we call it faith and patriotism!"

CHAPTER 42

During a few moments of their lives, ordinary real people, people real as a tooth-brush, do actually transcend the coarsely physical aspects of sex and feeding, and do approximate to the unwavering glow of romantic heroes.

CHAPTER 42

Carl Ericson on not procreating: "Maybe a thousand years from now, when every one is so artistic that they want to write books, it will be hard to get enough drudges. But now—Look at any office, with the clerks toiling day after day, even the unmarried ones. Look at all the young fathers of families, giving up everything they want to do, to support children who'll do the same thing right over again with their children. Always handing on the torch of life, but never getting any light from it. People don't run away from slavery often enough. And so they don't ever get to do real work, either!"

CHAPTER 42

Carl Ericson: "How bully it is to be living, if you don't have to give up living in order to make a living."

The Job: An American Novel (1917)

Sinclair Lewis has found his voice! Though he will deviate away from it every now and then, *The Job* undeniably taught the author how it felt to be true to himself. He must have been extremely proud of this novel–that pride shows itself in the text. My only personal regret about *The Job* is that it wasn't a massive commercial hit. While *Main Street* truly is brilliant and deserved its success, and even though *The Job* is less brilliant, it still deserved more attention than it received in 1917.

The problem with *The Job* is its subject matter: a successful businesswoman of the early twentieth century. The people of the time were simply not ready to know about the struggles of working women in America. Lewis doesn't hold anything back in *The Job*, as his exhaustive research pours onto the pages. The low wages, the politics, the begging for raises, the boredom, the male egos, the intense sexual harassment–it's all in this novel. We can hardly face these realities today, let alone how we would have felt facing them in 1917.

The Job is the story of Una Golden. Nothing comes easy for this small-town girl whose life is not occurring the way she hoped. She must either take action or starve. Unfortunately, the entire system is designed to work against her and the thousands of other single women who find themselves struggling to survive in New York City. Even worse is the fact that landing a job brings with it anxiety and the boredom of routine. Often, for women like Una, the only escapes are marriage and death–sometimes both together.

Una Golden is the first of Sinclair Lewis's strong female main characters. We will meet many more as we continue through his work. I often wonder how he was able to create such complete characterizations of strong working women at a time when these women were entirely ignored. Perhaps it was a combination of his prolific observation skills and the strong women that surrounded him in his personal life. At the time of writing *The Job*, Lewis's influential stepmother Isabel was still alive. Also, three years earlier, he had married Grace Hegger. Grace was no stranger to the world of New York office politics—she was an editor at *Vogue* when Lewis met her in a New York City elevator.

Other main themes of the book are the pursuit to find a balance between life and work, and to resist the notion that life is only defined by work. Sadly, these are pursuits we still struggle with today. In America, especially, our identities continue to focus on "the job".

CHAPTER 1
On Lew Golden: He believed that all Parisians, artists, millionaires, and socialists were immoral. His entire system of theology was comprised in the Bible, which he never read, and the Methodist Church, which he rarely attended; and he desired no system of economics beyond the current platform of the Republican Party.

CHAPTER 1
One of the most familiar human combinations in the world is that of unemployed daughter and widowed mother. A thousand times you have seen the jobless daughter devoting all of her curiosity, all of her youth, to a widowed mother of small pleasantries, a small income, and a shabby security. Thirty comes, and thirty-five. The daughter ages steadily. At forty she is as old as her unwithering mother.

CHAPTER 1
Una Golden: "If I were only a boy," sighed Una, "I could go to work in the hardware-store or on the railroad or anywhere, and not lose respectability. Oh, I *hate* being a woman."

CHAPTER 3

Her father's death had freed her; had permitted her to toil for her mother, cherish her, be regarded as useful. Instantly–still without learning that there was such a principle as feminism–she had become a feminist, demanding the world and all the fullness thereof as her field of labor.

CHAPTER 3

The sadness of it tortured Una while she was realizing that her mother had lost all practical comprehension of the details of life, was become a child, trusting everything to her daughter, yet retaining a power of suffering such as no child can know.

CHAPTER 4

There is plenty of romance in business. Fine, large, meaningless, general terms like romance and business can always be related. They take the place of thinking, and are highly useful to optimists and lecturers. But in the world of business there is a bewildered new Muse of Romance, who is clad not in silvery tissue of dreams, but in a neat blue suit that won't grow too shiny under the sleeves.

CHAPTER 4

On the world of business: It compels men whom it has never seen to toil in distant factories and produce useless wares, which are never actually brought into the office, but which it nevertheless sells to the heathen in the Solomon Islands in exchange for commodities whose very names it does not know; and in order to perform this miracle of transmutation it keeps stenographers so busy that they change from dewy girls into tight-lipped spinsters before they discover life.

CHAPTER 4

And our heroine is important not because she is an Amazon or a Ramona, but because she is representative of some millions of women in business, and because, in a vague but undiscouraged way, she keeps on inquiring what women in business can do to make human their existence of loveless routine.

CHAPTER 6

Then Una began to ponder the problem which is so weighty to girls of the city—where she could see her lover, since the parks were impolite and her own home obtrusively dull to him.

CHAPTER 7

There are times in any perplexed love when the lovers revel in bringing out just those problems and demands and complaints which they have most carefully concealed. At such a time of mutual confession, if the lovers are honest and tender, there is none of the abrasive hostility of a vulgar quarrel. But the kindliness of the review need not imply that it is profitable; often it ends, as it began, with the wail, "What can we do?" But so much alike are all the tribe of lovers, that the debaters never fail to stop now and then to congratulate themselves on being so frank!

CHAPTER 8

She was an Average Young Woman on a Job; she thought in terms of money and offices; yet she was one with all the men and women, young and old, who were creating a new age. She was nothing in herself, yet as the molecule of water belongs to the ocean, so Una Golden humbly belonged to the leaven who, however confusedly, were beginning to demand, "Why, since we have machinery, science, courage, need we go on tolerating war and poverty and caste and uncouthness, and all that sheer clumsiness?"

CHAPTER 9

The Grays took Una in as though she were their guest, but they did not bother her. They were city-born, taught by the city to let other people live their own lives.

CHAPTER 11

Mrs. Fike, during a rooming house interview: "What's your denomination?... No agnostics or Catholics allowed!"

Main Speak: Quotes from the Work of Sinclair Lewis

CHAPTER 13

Una was tired, but the morning's radiance inspired her. "My America—so beautiful! Why do we turn you into stuffy offices and ugly towns?" she marveled while she was dressing.

CHAPTER 13

Eddie Schwirtz: "Nother thing: I never could figger out what all these socialists and I. W. W.'s, these 'I Won't Work's, would do if we did divide up and hand all the industries over to them. I bet they'd be the very first ones to kick for a return to the old conditions! I tell you, it surprises me when a good, bright man like Jack London or this fella, Upton Sinclair—they say he's a well-educated fella, too—don't stop and realize these things."

CHAPTER 13

Una, on vacation: She thought of the momently more horrible fact that vacation was over, that the office would engulf her again. She declared to herself that two weeks were just long enough holiday to rest her, to free her from the office; not long enough to begin to find positive joy.

CHAPTER 14

After more than a month, during which Mr. Ross diverted himself by making appointments, postponing them, forgetting them, telephoning, telegraphing, sending special-delivery letters, being paged at hotels, and doing all the useless melodramatic things he could think of, except using an aeroplane or a submarine, he decided to make her his secretary at twenty dollars a week.

CHAPTER 14

On Mr. Ross: He was fond of the word "smart." "Rather smart poster, eh?" he would say, holding up the latest creation of his genius—that is to say, of his genius in hiring the men who had planned and prepared the creation.

CHAPTER 14

She could not imagine any future for these women in business except the accidents of marriage or death—or a revolution in the attitude toward them. She saw that the comfortable average men of the office sooner or later, if they were but faithful and lived long enough, had opportunities, responsibility, forced upon them. No such force was used upon the comfortable average women! She endeavored to picture a future in which women, the ordinary, philoprogenitive, unambitious women, would have some way out besides being married off or killed off. She envisioned a complete change in the fundamental purpose of organized business from the increased production of soap—or books or munitions—to the increased production of happiness.

CHAPTER 15

On Eddie Schwirtz: Apparently he was proud of his God-given body—though it had been slightly bloated since God had given it to him—and wanted to inspire her not only with the artistic vision of it, but with his care for it.... His thick woolen undergarments were so uncompromisingly wooleny.

CHAPTER 17

If any one moment of life is more important than the others, this may have been her crisis, when her husband had become a begging pauper and she took charge; began not only to think earnest, commonplace, little Una thoughts about "mastering life," but actually to master it.

CHAPTER 21

Mr. Fein on the terrible business of Business: "Good Lord! of course it's bad. But do you know anything in this world that isn't bad—that's anywhere near perfect? Except maybe Bach fugues? Religion, education, medicine, war, agriculture, art, pleasure, anything—all systems are choked with clumsy, outworn methods and ignorance—the whole human race works and plays at about ten-per-cent. efficiency."

CHAPTER 22

On Una finding her voice: She sailed up to a corner table by a window. The waiter gave the menu to Mr. Sidney, but she held out her hand for it. "This is my lunch. I'm a business woman, not just a woman," she said to Mr. Sidney; and she rapidly ordered a lunch which was shockingly imitative of one which Mr. Fein had once ordered for her.

CHAPTER 23

Una: "I will keep my job—if I've had this world of offices wished on to me, at least I'll conquer it, and give my clerks a decent time," the business woman meditated. "But just the same—oh, I am a woman, and I do need love."

Michael Fridgen

The Innocents: A Story for Lovers (1917)

The Innocents is a delightful little gem. I really hate writing that because no Sinclair Lewis novel should ever be considered delightful, little, or gem-like. But that's how I feel about *The Innocents*. In many ways, the book is less like Sinclair Lewis and more like a really long short story by O. Henry. (With a few situations thrown in that O. Henry would never have dared mention, namely, suicide and burglary.)

I like to think that Lewis, at this point in his career, was much like a lioness about to pounce. *The Job* made him realize what he was capable of accomplishing. However, just like the lioness before she strikes, he needed to become very still, gather strength, and conserve energy. He was about to attack the 1920's with the greatest literary force America had ever seen. Lewis was writing in order to feed his family, and at the same time he was saving his intellectual strength to fuel the approaching hunt.

The Innocents is unlike a Sinclair Lewis novel because the central relationship contains no turmoil. Mother and Father Appleby are in their sixties and adorably in love. The rely on each other because they truly trust each other. There is no irony in the Appleby relationship. Also, unlike most of Lewis's other work, the heroes in *The Innocents* are rewarded and the villains get their comeuppance.

The story involves Mother and Father Appleby as they navigate aging in a society that owes nothing to practically anyone. In a time well before Social Security, we see the Appleby's get overlooked to the point of starvation.

But like a typical work by Lewis, a social issue is explored and dissected: ageism. Ageism is not a new phenomenon for our modern time of social media. In fact, this type of discrimination was much worse for centuries before the word became known. Aging people were, literally, discarded when they could no longer fight the daily grind. While the literal has become, hopefully, more figurative today, the pain is no less as great.

CHAPTER 1

On Father Appleby's attempt to be granted vacation time: So every year it was necessary for Father to develop a cough, not much of a cough, merely a small, polite noise, like a mouse begging pardon of an irate bee, yet enough to talk about and win him a two weeks' leave. Every year he schemed for this leave, and almost ruined his throat by sniffing snuff to make him sneeze.

CHAPTER 3

To Father there were only two kinds of tea—the kind you got for a nickel at the Automat, and the kind that Mother privately consumed. But here he had to choose intelligently among orange pekoe, oolong, Ceylon, and English-breakfast teas.

CHAPTER 3

Ye Tea Shoppe was artistic. You could tell that by the fact that none of the arts and crafts wares exposed for sale were in the least useful. And it was too artistic, too far above the sordidness of commercialism, to put any prices on the menu-cards. Consequently Father was worried about his bill all the time he was encouraging his guests to forget their uncomfortably decorative surroundings and talk like regular people.

CHAPTER 4

On moving out of New York: She felt that she was giving up ever so many metropolitan advantages by leaving New York so prematurely. Why, she'd never been inside Grant's Tomb! She'd miss her second cousin—not that she'd seen the cousin for a year or two.

CHAPTER 6

On the Appleby's grown daughter planning a visit: Lulu had informed them two weeks beforehand that they were to be honored with the presence of herself and her son Harry; and Father and Mother had been unable to think of any excuse strong enough to keep her away. Lulu wasn't unkind to her parents; rather, she was too kind; she gave them good advice and tried to arrange Mother's hair in the coiffures displayed by Mrs. Edward Schuyler Deflaver of Saserkopee, who gave smart teas at the Woman's Exchange. Lulu cheerily told Father how well he was withstanding the hand of Time, which made him feel decrepit and become profane.

CHAPTER 8

Having once admitted hopelessness, it was humanly natural that they should again hope that they hoped.

CHAPTER 9

On the Appleby's grown daughter: It may seem a mystery as to why a woman whose soul was composed of vinegar and chicken feathers, as was Lulu Appleby Hartwig's, should have wanted her parents to stay with her. Perhaps she liked them. One does find such anomalies.

CHAPTER 10

Father Appleby on Mother getting a job: "Why–why–you don't need–I don't know as I like–" began the conventional old Father to whom woman's place was in the home whether or not there was a home in which to have a place. Then the new Father, the adventurer, declared, "I think it's mighty fine, Mother. Mighty fine. If it won't be too hard on you."

CHAPTER 13

It's always easier to be a bold adventurer in some town other than the one in which you are.

CHAPTER 13

On a nameless woman who fed the Appleby's: Mother and he were, to this woman, a proof that freedom and love and distant skies did actually exist, and that people, just folks, not rich, could go and find them.

CHAPTER 14

Most people do not know why they do things—not even you and I invariably know, though of course we are superior to the unresponsive masses. Many people are even unconscious that they are doing things or being things—being gentle or cruel or creative or parasitic. Quite without knowing it, Father was searching for his place in the world. The New York shoe-stores had decided that he was too old to be useful. But age is as fictitious as time or love.

CHAPTER 14

It is earnestly recommended to all uncomfortable or dissatisfied men over sixty that they take their wives and their mouth-organs and go tramping in winter, whether they be bank presidents or shoe-clerks or writers of fiction or just plain honest men. Though doubtless some of them may have difficulty in getting their wives to go.

Michael Fridgen

Free Air (1919)

It's quite fitting that *Free Air* was Sinclair Lewis's last book
before *Main Street*. *Free Air* is about enduring a journey in order to discover the wonders of a destination. With his writing
career, this is what Lewis has done. He's endured harsh professors, lack of sales, critical reviews, some hunger, and many
folks who thought it was time he should get a real job. Now,
with the release of *Free Air*, his destination is right around the
corner.

The journey depicted in *Free Air* is both literal and figurative. Clair Boltwood has persuaded her widowed father to ac-
company her as they drive across the country to Seattle. That's
the literal voyage. The figurative trip involves a young man that
they meet along the way: Milt Daggett. While the metaphor
between rough travel and a burgeoning relationship is not
new, it's still fun to read.

The most fascinating part of the novel is learning about
road trips at a time when roads were barely a thing. I believe
that nothing changed our culture more than the automobile. While the smartphone changed *how* we do things, cars
changed *what* we do. Horses were great for thousands of years,
but they couldn't match the practicality of the automobile.

Sinclair Lewis, born in 1885, was at just the right time in
history to experience early automobile travel. *Free Air* is full of
many examples of the trials faced by earlier motorists–these
people were no less brave or heroic than the early ocean ex-
plorers. The cars of the era broke down constantly. They were
always running out of gas with no filling station in sight. Often, two ruts through the prairie was all the road they had,
but at least that was better than the mud. During those early

decades, most roadside services were offered by scoundrels who wanted to rip-off unsuspecting amateurs. It's a wonder anybody got anywhere. (I mean this last sentence both literally and figuratively!)

We can surmise that Lewis was well into writing *Main Street* as he continued to work on *Free Air*–Gopher Prairie, Minnesota, the setting of *Main Street*, is featured in *Free Air*. We also, once again, hear about Joralemon, the home of Carl "Hawk" Ericson from *The Trail of the Hawk*. Milt Daggett, one of *Free Air*'s protagonists, is from Schoenstrom, Minnesota. We'll also hear more about Schoenstrom in Lewis's coming work.

I love thinking about Sinclair Lewis and his young wife Grace as they drove from New York to Sauk Centre, Minnesota. Where did they sleep? Where did they bathe? How did they smell? (Forgive me, as a writer I can't ignore these things.) I hope they got lost a few times. In my experience, getting lost is the best way to learn. Surely, if we learn anything from *Free Air*, Mr. and Mrs. Lewis must have broken down at least five times. I imagine that the brilliant author had to swallow his pride and beg a small-town mechanic for assistance. (Well...mechanics aren't cheap, and cars don't run on Nobel Prizes.)

CHAPTER 2

Claire had gone to a good school out of Philadelphia, on the Main Line. She was used to gracious leisure, attractive uselessness, nut-center chocolates, and a certain wonder as to why she was alive.

CHAPTER 3

Now of all the cosmic problems yet unsolved, not cancer nor the future of poverty are the flustering questions, but these twain: Which is worse, not to wear evening clothes at a party at which you find every one else dressed, or to come in evening clothes to a house where, it proves, they are never worn? And: Which is worse, not to tip when a tip has been expected; or to tip, when the tip is an insult?

CHAPTER 4

The state of mind of the touring motorist entering a strange place at night is as peculiar and definite as that of a prospector. It is compounded of gratitude at having got safely in; of perception of a new town, yet with all eagerness about new things dulled by weariness; of hope that there is going to be a good hotel, but small expectation—and absolutely no probability—that there really will be one.

CHAPTER 5

Milt was the most prosperous young man in the village of Schoenstrom. Neither the village itself nor the nearby Strom is really schoen.

CHAPTER 6

No longer was she haunted by the apprehension that had whispered to her as she had left Minneapolis. She knew a thrill when she hailed—as though it were a passing ship—an Illinois car across whose dust-caked back was a banner "Chicago to the Yellowstone." She experienced a new sensation of common humanness when, on a railway paralleling the wagon road for miles, the engineer of a freight waved his hand to her, and tooted the whistle in greeting.

CHAPTER 7

Claire Boltwood on a chicken she passed along the road: "I'm not so sure," she meditated, while she absently watched another member of the Poultry Suicide Club rush out of a safe ditch, prepare to take leave for immortality, change her fowlish mind, flutter up over the hood of the car, and come down squawking her indignities to the barnyard.

CHAPTER 11

So for two hours Claire and her father experienced that most distressing of motor experiences—waiting, while the afternoon that would have been so good for driving went by them. Every fifteen minutes they came in from sitting on a dry-goods box in front of the garage, and never did the repair appear to be any farther along.

Main Speak: Quotes from the Work of Sinclair Lewis

CHAPTER 16

Claire's father, Mr. Boltwood: "I'd rather have one of these homesteads and look across my fields at those hills than be King of England." Not that he made any effort to buy one of the homesteads. But then, he made no appreciable effort to become King of England.

CHAPTER 18

Claire Boltwood: "Oh, it's all very well to talk, and be so superior about these dear old grandeurs of Nature, and the heroism of pioneers, and I do like a glimpse of them. But the niceties of life do mean something and even if it is weak and dependent, I shall always simply adore them!"

CHAPTER 20

Milt Daggett: "Let me remind you that Brer Julius Cæsar said he'd rather be mayor in a little Spanish town than police commissioner in Rome. I'm king in Schoenstrom, while you're just one of a couple hundred thousand bright people in New York–"

CHAPTER 24

Yes, she was glad that she had made the experiment–but gladder that she was safely in from the long dust-whitened way, back in her own world of beauty; and she couldn't imagine ever trying it again.

CHAPTER 25

On Milt Daggett's feelings toward Claire Boltwood: Not once did he stop to consider how glorious it would be to marry Claire–or how terrifying it would be to marry Miss Boltwood.

CHAPTER 26

The American state universities admit, in a pleased way, that though Yale and Harvard and Princeton may be snobbish, the state universities are the refuge of a myth called "college democracy." But there is no university near a considerable city into which the inheritors of the wealth of that city do not carry all the local social distinctions. Their family rank, their place in the unwritten peerage, determines to which fraternity they shall be elected, and the fraternity determines with whom—men and girls—they shall be intimate.

CHAPTER 31

On Milt Daggett: He had received from Mrs. Gilson a note inviting him to share their box at the first night of a three-night Opera Season. He had spent half a day in trying to think of a courteously rude way of declining.

CHAPTER 31

West of Chicago, "You bet" means "Rather," and "Yes indeed," and "On the whole I should be inclined to fancy that there may be some vestiges of accuracy in your curious opinion," and "You're a liar but I can't afford to say so."

CHAPTER 34

This is the beginning of the story of Milt and Claire Daggett. The prelude over and the curtain risen on the actual play, they face the anxieties and glories of a changing world. Not without quarrels and barren hours, not free from ignorance and the discomfort of finding that between the mountain peaks they must for long gray periods dwell in the dusty valleys, they yet start their drama with the distinction of being able to laugh together, with the advantage of having discovered that neither Schoenstrom nor Brooklyn Heights is quite all of life, with the cosmic importance to the tedious world of believing in the romance that makes youth unquenchable.

Main Street (1920)

Here it is: Sinclair Lewis's most popular work and the one that inspired my love affair with him. During my first reading of the novel in the mid-1990's, I simply could not put it down. *Main Street* continues to have the same appeal for me during several readings since that time. Each time I read this book I discover new insights into the world of Gopher Prairie, Minnesota.

Sinclair Lewis's real hometown of Sauk Centre, Minnesota served as the model for the fictional Gopher Prairie. Today, signs proclaim Sauk Centre's Main Street as 'The Original Main Street.' The heart of the actual town is the intersection of Main Street and Sinclair Lewis Avenue. Heading on Main Street toward Sauk Lake, take a left on Sinclair Lewis Avenue to visit the home where the future author spent his entire childhood. Taking a right on Sinclair Lewis Avenue will bring you directly to his grave site.

Main Street was a phenomenal success, to say the least. The book was enormously popular in large cities across the nation. In small towns, it was a different story. *Main Street* offended the residents of Sauk Centre. In the neighboring town of Alexandria, the novel was banned through a decree from the city council because it was thought to be un-American. (Alexandria has never admitted the irony of being a small town that banned a book which was about the ignorance of small towns that have the audacity to ban books!)

However, as the years went on, and Sinclair Lewis won the Nobel Prize, Sauk Centre changed its mind and embraced their favorite son. The Lewis home is open for tours and the lovely Sinclair Lewis Park sits along the shores of Sauk Lake.

The author is the subject of two prominent murals painted on buildings in the town's small downtown. Sauk Centre High School's mascot is the Mainstreeters. (When I was a senior in high school, we played Sauk Centre for Homecoming. The theme for our Homecoming that year was "Rumble on Main Street." My senior class made a float that showed several of Sauk Centre's buildings being destroyed by a giant football. Sinclair Lewis would surely have approved of the destruction but disapproved of the general concept of football.)

The premise of the book is, basically, a fish-out-of-water story. However, there is nothing basic about the main characters–suddenly, this simple theme becomes complex, frustrating, humorous, and sad. The story is centered on the life of Carol, a young librarian accustomed to the cities of Chicago, St. Paul, and Minneapolis. She marries Will Kennicott, a prairie doctor, and moves with him to his hometown of Gopher Prairie, Minnesota. There, she loves and hates her way through life.

Among the many themes found in *Main Street* is what Lewis calls the Village Virus. This illness infects the citizens of small towns and diminishes their faculties so that they enjoy their surroundings. Like the residents of Gopher Prairie, I have had the Village Virus. It is a real sickness and I'm sorry to admit that I fell victim to its terrible side effects.

Ultimately, I need to recognize that I know the people from the pages of *Main Street*–I've loved and hated them my whole life. At the same time, I absolutely hate to recognize that some negative parts of Main Street are also within me. Reading *Main Street* is a sort of therapy for me. I feel better knowing that someone else experienced small-town life in the way that I did. Just as relevant today as it was when published in 1920, *Main Street* is as brilliant as literature gets.

Main Speak: Quotes from the Work of Sinclair Lewis

CHAPTER 1 PART 2

Daily, on the library steps or in the hall of the Main Building, the co-eds talked of "What shall we do when we finish college?" Even the girls who knew that they were going to be married pretended to be considering important business positions; even they who knew that they would have to work hinted about fabulous suitors.

CHAPTER 1 PART 5

After graduation she never saw Stewart Snyder again. She wrote to him once a week–for one month.

CHAPTER 2 PART 2

Dr. Will Kennicott: "Come on. Come to Gopher Prairie. Show us. Make the town–well–make it artistic. It's mighty pretty, but I'll admit we aren't any too darn artistic. Probably the lumber-yard isn't as scrumptious as all these Greek temples. But go to it! Make us change!"

CHAPTER 3 PART 3

Carol Kennicott: "I love you for understanding. I'm just–I'm beastly over-sensitive. Too many books. It's my lack of shoulder-muscles and sense. Give me time, dear."

CHAPTER 4 PART 1

She saw the furniture as a circle of elderly judges, condemning her to death by smothering. The tottering brocade chair squeaked, "Choke her–choke her–smother her." The old linen smelled of the tomb. She was alone in this house, this strange still house, among the shadows of dead thoughts and haunting repressions.

CHAPTER 4 PART 4

Dr. Will Kennicott: "Uh, Carrie–You ought to be more careful about shocking folks. Talking about gold stockings, and about showing your ankles to schoolteachers and all!"

CHAPTER 5 PART 2

Raymie Wutherspoon: "One trouble with books is that they're not so thoroughly safeguarded by intelligent censors as the movies are, and when you drop into the library and take out a book you never know what you're wasting your time on. What I like in books is a wholesome, really improving story, and sometimes–Why, once I started a novel by this fellow Balzac that you read about, and it told how a lady wasn't living with her husband, I mean she wasn't his wife. It went into details, disgustingly! And the English was real poor. I spoke to the library about it, and they took it off the shelves."

CHAPTER 7 PART 1

Winter is not a season in the North Middlewest; it is an industry.

CHAPTER 7 PART 2

She could not have outside employment. To the village doctor's wife it was taboo. She was a woman with a working brain and no work. There were only three things which she could do: Have children; start her career of reforming; or become so definitely a part of the town that she would be fulfilled by the activities of church and study-club and bridge-parties.

CHAPTER 9 PART 2

In her innocence she had not known that the whole town could discuss even her garments, her body. She felt that she was being dragged naked down Main Street.

CHAPTER 11 PART 8

Mrs. Mary Ellen Wilks: "If this class of people had an understanding of Science and that we are the children of God and nothing can harm us, they wouldn't be in error and poverty."

CHAPTER 12 PART 3

Virgins are not so virginal as they used to be.

CHAPTER 13 PART 1

Guy Pollock: "More dangerous than the cancer that will certainly get me at fifty unless I stop this smoking. The Village Virus is the germ which–it's extraordinarily like the hook-worm–it infects ambitious people who stay too long in the provinces. You'll find it epidemic among lawyers and doctors and ministers and college-bred merchants—all these people who have had a glimpse of the world that thinks and laughs, but have returned to their swamp. I'm a perfect example. But I sha'n't pester you with my dolors."

CHAPTER 13 PART 1

Guy Pollock: "I decided to leave here. Stern resolution. Grasp the world. Then I found that the Village Virus had me, absolute: I didn't want to face new streets and younger men—real competition. It was too easy to go on making out conveyances and arguing ditching cases. So—That's all of the biography of a living dead man, except the diverting last Chapter, the lies about my having been 'a tower of strength and legal wisdom' which some day a preacher will spin over my lean dry body."

CHAPTER 15 PART 7

Mrs. Bogart went thoroughly into the rumor that the girl waiter at Billy's Lunch was not all she might be—or, rather, was quite all she might be.

CHAPTER 15 PART 7

Carol Kennicott on Mrs. Bogart: "If that woman is on the side of the angels, then I have no choice; I must be on the side of the devil. But—isn't she like me? She too wants to 'reform the town'! She too criticizes everybody! She too thinks the men are vulgar and limited! AM I LIKE HER? This is ghastly!"

CHAPTER 17 PART 2

On the Gopher Prairie Dramatic Club: Of these fifteen only seven came to the first meeting. The rest telephoned their unparalleled regrets and engagements and illnesses, and announced that they would be present at all other meetings through eternity.

CHAPTER 19 PART 6

At the lake cottage she missed the passing of the trains. She realized that in town she had depended upon them for assurance that there remained a world beyond.

CHAPTER 19 PART 6
Even in this new era of motors the citizens went down to the station to see the trains go through. It was their romance; their only mystery besides mass at the Catholic Church.

CHAPTER 19 PART 8
Two weeks later the Great War smote Europe. For a month Gopher Prairie had the delight of shuddering, then, as the war settled down to a business of trench-fighting, they forgot.

CHAPTER 20 PART 1
Then the baby was born, without unusual difficulty: a boy with straight back and strong legs. The first day she hated him for the tides of pain and hopeless fear he had caused; she resented his raw ugliness. After that she loved him with all the devotion and instinct at which she had scoffed.

CHAPTER 20 PART 2
Carol Kennicott on her child's baptism (or lack there of): "I refuse to insult my baby and myself by asking an ignorant young man in a frock coat to sanction him, to permit me to have him! I refuse to subject him to any devil-chasing rites! If I didn't give my baby—MY BABY— enough sanctification in those nine hours of hell, then he can't get any more out of the Reverend Mr. Zitterel!"

CHAPTER 20 PART 2
The true Main Streetite defines a relative as a person to whose house you go uninvited, to stay as long as you like. If you hear that Lym Cass on his journey East has spent all his time "visiting" in Oyster Center, it does not mean that he prefers that village to the rest of New England, but that he has relatives there. It does not mean that he has written to the relatives these many years, nor that they have ever given signs of a desire to look upon him. But "you wouldn't expect a man to go and spend good money at a hotel in Boston, when his own third cousins live right in the same state, would you?"

Main Speak: Quotes from the Work of Sinclair Lewis

CHAPTER 22 PART 1

The greatest mystery about a human being is not his reaction to sex or praise, but the manner in which he contrives to put in twenty-four hours a day. It is this which puzzles the long-shoreman about the clerk, the Londoner about the bushman.

CHAPTER 22 PART 3

On life in a small town: It is an unimaginatively standardized background, a sluggishness of speech and manners, a rigid ruling of the spirit by the desire to appear respectable. It is contentment ... the contentment of the quiet dead, who are scornful of the living for their restless walking. It is negation canonized as the one positive virtue. It is the prohibition of happiness. It is slavery self-sought and self-defended. It is dullness made God. A savorless people, gulping tasteless food, and sitting afterward, coatless and thoughtless, in rocking-chairs prickly with inane decorations, listening to mechanical music, saying mechanical things about the excellence of Ford automobiles, and viewing themselves as the greatest race in the world.

CHAPTER 23 PART 5

Perce Bresnehan to Carol Kennicott: "My humble (not too humble!) opinion is that you like to be different. You like to think you're peculiar. Why, if you knew how many tens of thousands of women, especially in New York, say just what you do, you'd lose all the fun of thinking you're a lone genius and you'd be on the band-wagon whooping it up for Gopher Prairie and a good decent family life. There's always about a million young women just out of college who want to teach their grandmothers how to suck eggs."

CHAPTER 24 PART 5

She looked at the town. She saw that in adventuring from Main Street, Gopher Prairie, to Main Street, Joralemon, she had not stirred. There were the same two-story brick groceries with lodge-signs above the awnings; the same one-story wooden millinery shop; the same fire-brick garages; the same prairie at the open end of the wide street; the same people wondering whether the levity of eating a hot-dog sandwich would break their taboos.

CHAPTER 28 PART 2

Will Kennicott on religion: "Sure, religion is a fine influence–got to have it to keep the lower classes in order–fact, it's the only thing that appeals to a lot of those fellows and makes 'em respect the rights of property. And I guess this theology is O.K.; lot of wise old coots figured it all out, and they knew more about it than we do." He believed in the Christian religion, and never thought about it, he believed in the church, and seldom went near it; he was shocked by Carol's lack of faith, and wasn't quite sure what was the nature of the faith that she lacked.

CHAPTER 29 PART 6

Carol Kennicott: "I have become a small-town woman. Absolute. Typical. Modest and moral and safe. Protected from life. GENTEEL! The Village Virus–the village virtuousness. My hair–just scrambled together. What can Erik see in that wedded spinster there? He does like me! Because I'm the only woman who's decent to him! How long before he'll wake up to me? ... I've waked up to myself... . Am I as old as–as old as I am?"

CHAPTER 30 PART 2

In a passionate escape there must be not only a place from which to flee but a place to which to flee. She had known that she would gladly leave Gopher Prairie, leave Main Street and all that it signified, but she had had no destination.

CHAPTER 31 PART 2

There are two insults which no human being will endure: the assertion that he hasn't a sense of humor, and the doubly impertinent assertion that he has never known trouble.

CHAPTER 33 PART 1

Dr. Will Kennicott to Carol Kennicott: "No matter even if you are cold, I like you better than anybody in the world. One time I said that you were my soul. And that still goes. You're all the things that I see in a sunset when I'm driving in from the country, the things that I like but can't make poetry of. Do you realize what my job is? I go round twenty-four hours a day, in mud and blizzard, trying my damnedest to heal everybody, rich or poor. You—that 're always spieling about how scientists ought to rule the world, instead of a bunch of spread-eagle politicians—can't you see that I'm all the science there is here? And I can stand the cold and the bumpy roads and the lonely rides at night. All I need is to have you here at home to welcome me. I don't expect you to be passionate—not any more I don't—but I do expect you to appreciate my work. I bring babies into the world, and save lives, and make cranky husbands quit being mean to their wives. And then you go and moon over a Swede tailor because he can talk about how to put ruchings on a skirt! Hell of a thing for a man to fuss over!"

CHAPTER 34 PART 1

Her only struggle was in coaxing Kennicott not to spend all his time with the tourists from the ten thousand other Gopher Prairies. In winter, California is full of people from Iowa and Nebraska, Ohio and Oklahoma, who, having traveled thousands of miles from their familiar villages, hasten to secure an illusion of not having left them. They hunt for people from their own states to stand between them and the shame of naked mountains; they talk steadily, in Pullmans, on hotel porches, at cafeterias and motion-picture shows, about the motors and crops and county politics back home.

CHAPTER 36 PART 3

She had her freedom, and it was empty. The moment was not the highest of her life, but the lowest and most desolate, which was altogether excellent, for instead of slipping downward she began to climb.

CHAPTER 37 PART 5

The chart which plots Carol's progress is not easy to read. The lines are broken and uncertain of direction; often instead of rising they sink in wavering scrawls; and the colors are watery blue and pink and the dim gray of rubbed pencil marks. A few lines are traceable.

CHAPTER 37 PART 5

And why, she began to ask, did she rage at individuals? Not individuals but institutions are the enemies, and they most afflict the disciples who the most generously serve them. They insinuate their tyranny under a hundred guises and pompous names, such as Polite Society, the Family, the Church, Sound Business, the Party, the Country, the Superior White Race; and the only defense against them, Carol beheld, is unembittered laughter.

CHAPTER 38 PART 8

Unnamed leader of suffrage movement to Carol Kennicott: "It must have been so easy in the good old days when authors dreamed only of selling a hundred thousand volumes, and sculptors of being feted in big houses, and even the Uplifters like me had a simple-hearted ambition to be elected to important offices and invited to go round lecturing. But we meddlers have upset everything. Now the one thing that is disgraceful to any of us is obvious success. The Uplifter who is very popular with wealthy patrons can be pretty sure that he has softened his philosophy to please them, and the author who is making lots of money—poor things, I've heard 'em apologizing for it to the shabby bitter-enders; I've seen 'em ashamed of the sleek luggage they got from movie rights. Do you want to sacrifice yourself in such a topsy-turvy world, where popularity makes you unpopular with the people you love, and the only failure is cheap success, and the only individualist is the person who gives up all his individualism to serve a jolly ungrateful proletariat which thumbs its nose at him?"

CHAPTER 38 PART 9

Carol Kennicott: "I've been making the town a myth. This is how people keep up the tradition of the perfect home-town, the happy boyhood, the brilliant college friends. We forget so. I've been forgetting that Main Street doesn't think it's in the least lonely and pitiful. It thinks it's God's Own Country. It isn't waiting for me. It doesn't care."

CHAPTER 39 PART 5

Her baby, born in August, was a girl. Carol could not decide whether she was to become a feminist leader or marry a scientist or both, but did settle on Vassar and a tricolette suit with a small black hat for her Freshman year.

CHAPTER 39 PART 8

On Carol Kennicott's dream for the future: She led him to the nursery door, pointed at the fuzzy brown head of her daughter. "Do you see that object on the pillow? Do you know what it is? It's a bomb to blow up smugness. If you Tories were wise, you wouldn't arrest anarchists; you'd arrest all these children while they're asleep in their cribs. Think what that baby will see and meddle with before she dies in the year 2000! She may see an industrial union of the whole world, she may see aeroplanes going to Mars."

CHAPTER 39 PART 8

Carol Kennicott: "But I have won in this: I've never excused my failures by sneering at my aspirations, by pretending to have gone beyond them. I do not admit that Main Street is as beautiful as it should be! I do not admit that Gopher Prairie is greater or more generous than Europe! I do not admit that dish-washing is enough to satisfy all women! I may not have fought the good fight, but I have kept the faith."

Babbitt (1922)

I stated earlier that *Main Street* was as brilliant as literature gets. But then Sinclair Lewis went and wrote *Babbitt*. He captured the life of this businessman so well that I feel I intimately know the lives of all realtors, stockbrokers, and anyone who sells anything for a living. (As a feminist, I also firmly believe that, yes, a woman could be a babbitt.)

The character of George Babbitt was so popular in the early 1920's that he became a word. In fact, it's still in the dictionary. The New Oxford American Dictionary defines the word babbitt as a noun for a materialistic, complacent, and conformist businessman. (A derivative, babbittry, is also acceptable.) We don't really use the word any longer–I reserve it exclusively for people I see in airport lounges and mid-priced chain restaurants.

It's quite sad that *Babbitt* has fallen into obscurity. Authors that win the Nobel Prize for Literature do not win for a specific book, but rather for their collective works. However, when Sinclair Lewis won the prize in 1930, the Nobel committee specifically mentioned *Babbitt* as Lewis's crowning achievement.

The thing that strikes me so profoundly about *Babbitt* is that if it had been written last year it would be basically the same. *Main Street* would have changed a bit due to the advent of the internet. The folks of Gopher Prairie, even those most sheltered, would still have been exposed to far-off places and ideas. But give George Babbitt the internet and his character would not change. In fact, George Babbitt's resolve to be a babbitt would be stronger with the reinforcement of like-minded people on social media.

Main Speak: Quotes from the Work of Sinclair Lewis

Babbitt lives in Zenith, a city that makes an appearance in several of Sinclair Lewis's most popular works. Zenith is a city of 361,000 in the Midwestern state of Winnemac. It's a fairly good-sized city for 1922. We know that Winnemac also includes another city of similar size, named Monarch (population 300,000). The capital of Winnemac is Galop de Vache, which is 'galloping cow' in French. We discover in *Elmer Gantry* that the state of Winnemac is somewhere between Pittsburgh and Chicago. In *Arrowsmith* we learn that Winnemac shares a border with Ohio, Indiana, Illinois, and Michigan.

I believe I like *Babbitt* so much because it makes me feel good about the choices I've made in my life. By choosing art, authenticity, and non-conformity, I can, hopefully, avoid the depression of "Good Ole Georgie". *Babbitt* also gives me empathy for the loud annoying guy next to me on an airplane that is the most important person in the world because he alone is a distributor of automobile tires. I can put up with his annoying babble because I know what his personal life is like; I feel sorrow for him, and due to my own personality defect, I feel better about myself.

CHAPTER 1 PART 2

His name was George F. Babbitt. He was forty-six years old now, in April, 1920, and he made nothing in particular, neither butter nor shoes nor poetry, but he was nimble in the calling of selling houses for more than people could afford to pay.

CHAPTER 1 PART 3

Then George F. Babbitt did a dismaying thing. He wiped his face on the guest-towel! It was a pansy-embroidered trifle which always hung there to indicate that the Babbitts were in the best Floral Heights society. No one had ever used it. No guest had ever dared to. Guests secretively took a corner of the nearest regular towel.

Michael Fridgen

CHAPTER 1 PART 4

George Babbitt on his daughter, Verona: "Ever since she got out of college she's been too rambunctious to live with—doesn't know what she wants—well, I know what she wants!—all she wants is to marry a millionaire, and live in Europe, and hold some preacher's hand, and simultaneously at the same time stay right here in Zenith and be some blooming kind of a socialist agitator or boss charity-worker or some damn thing!"

CHAPTER 2 PART 1

In fact there was but one thing wrong with the Babbitt house: It was not a home.

CHAPTER 3 PART 3

On George Babbitt and his thoughts about infidelity: For all his wandering thoughts, they had never been more intimate than this. He often reflected, "Nev' forget how old Jake Offutt said a wise bird never goes love-making in his own office or his own home. Start trouble."

CHAPTER 4 PART 3

On George Babbitt and smoking: He stopped smoking at least once a month. He went through with it like the solid citizen he was: admitted the evils of tobacco, courageously made resolves, laid out plans to check the vice, tapered off his allowance of cigars, and expounded the pleasures of virtuousness to every one he met. He did everything, in fact, except stop smoking.

CHAPTER 4 PART 4

George Babbitt: "A good labor union is of value because it keeps out radical unions, which would destroy property. No one ought to be forced to belong to a union, however. All labor agitators who try to force men to join a union should be hanged. In fact, just between ourselves, there oughtn't to be any unions allowed at all; and as it's the best way of fighting the unions, every business man ought to belong to an employers'-association and to the Chamber of Commerce. In union there is strength. So any selfish hog who doesn't join the Chamber of Commerce ought to be forced to."

CHAPTER 4 PART 4

George Babbitt on selling real estate: "Course I don't mean to say that every ad I write is literally true or that I always believe everything I say when I give some buyer a good strong selling-spiel. You see—you see it's like this: In the first place, maybe the owner of the property exaggerated when he put it into my hands, and it certainly isn't my place to go proving my principal a liar! And then most folks are so darn crooked themselves that they expect a fellow to do a little lying, so if I was fool enough to never whoop the ante I'd get the credit for lying anyway!"

CHAPTER 5 PART 1

Babbitt's preparations for leaving the office to its feeble self during the hour and a half of his lunch-period were somewhat less elaborate than the plans for a general European war.

CHAPTER 5 PART 2

The effect of his scientific budget-planning was that he felt at once triumphantly wealthy and perilously poor, and in the midst of these dissertations he stopped his car, rushed into a small news-and-miscellany shop, and bought the electric cigar-lighter which he had coveted for a week.

CHAPTER 5 PART 3

Paul Riesling: "Take all these fellows we know, the kind right here in the club now, that seem to be perfectly content with their home-life and their businesses, and that boost Zenith and the Chamber of Commerce and holler for a million population. I bet if you could cut into their heads you'd find that one-third of 'em are sure-enough satisfied with their wives and kids and friends and their offices; and one-third feel kind of restless but won't admit it; and one-third are miserable and know it. They hate the whole peppy, boosting, go-ahead game, and they're bored by their wives and think their families are fools—at least when they come to forty or forty-five they're bored—and they hate business, and they'd go–Why do you suppose there's so many 'mysterious' suicides? Why do you suppose so many Substantial Citizens jumped right into the war? Think it was all patriotism?"

CHAPTER 6 PART 3

On George Babbitt's views: Furthermore, he felt that on the subject of Shakespeare he wasn't really an authority. Neither the Advocate-Times, the Evening Advocate, nor the Bulletin of the Zenith Chamber of Commerce had ever had an editorial on the matter, and until one of them had spoken he found it hard to form an original opinion.

CHAPTER 7 PART 3

It was his luxurious custom to shave while sitting snugly in a tubful of hot water. He may be viewed to-night as a plump, smooth, pink, baldish, podgy goodman, robbed of the importance of spectacles, squatting in breast-high water, scraping his lather-smeared cheeks with a safety-razor like a tiny lawn-mower, and with melancholy dignity clawing through the water to recover a slippery and active piece of soap.

CHAPTER 7 PART 3

Just as he was an Elk, a Booster, and a member of the Chamber of Commerce, just as the priests of the Presbyterian Church determined his every religious belief and the senators who controlled the Republican Party decided in little smoky rooms in Washington what he should think about disarmament, tariff, and Germany, so did the large national advertisers fix the surface of his life, fix what he believed to be his individuality. These standard advertised wares–toothpastes, socks, tires, cameras, instantaneous hot-water heaters–were his symbols and proofs of excellence; at first the signs, then the substitutes, for joy and passion and wisdom.

CHAPTER 7 PART 4

At that moment a G. A. R. veteran was dying. He had come from the Civil War straight to a farm which, though it was officially within the city-limits of Zenith, was primitive as the backwoods. He had never ridden in a motor car, never seen a bath-tub, never read any book save the Bible, McGuffey's readers, and religious tracts; and he believed that the earth is flat, that the English are the Lost Ten Tribes of Israel, and that the United States is a democracy.

CHAPTER 9 PART 2

On George Babbitt's plan to vacation without his wife: For many minutes, for many hours, for a bleak eternity, he lay awake, shivering, reduced to primitive terror, comprehending that he had won freedom, and wondering what he could do with anything so unknown and so embarrassing as freedom.

CHAPTER 12 PART 2

He honestly believed that he loved baseball. It is true that he hadn't, in twenty-five years, himself played any baseball except back-lot catch with Ted—very gentle, and strictly limited to ten minutes. But the game was a custom of his clan, and it gave outlet for the homicidal and sides-taking instincts which Babbitt called "patriotism" and "love of sport."

CHAPTER 13 PART 5

The meetings of the convention were held in the ballroom of the Allen House. In an anteroom was the office of the chairman of the executive committee. He was the busiest man in the convention; he was so busy that he got nothing done whatever.

CHAPTER 13 PART 5

On a party given for the delegates to the state convention of realtors: The guests drove off; the garden shivered into quiet. But Mrs. Crosby Knowlton sighed as she looked at a marble seat warm from five hundred summers of Amalfi. On the face of a winged sphinx which supported it someone had drawn a mustache in lead-pencil. Crumpled paper napkins were dumped among the Michaelmas daisies. On the walk, like shredded lovely flesh, were the petals of the last gallant rose. Cigarette stubs floated in the goldfish pool, trailing an evil stain as they swelled and disintegrated, and beneath the marble seat, the fragments carefully put together, was a smashed teacup.

CHAPTER 15 PART 5

He accepted Overbrook's next plaintive invitation, for an evening two weeks off. A dinner two weeks off, even a family dinner, never seems so appalling, till the two weeks have astoundingly disappeared and one comes dismayed to the ambushed hour.

CHAPTER 16 PART 3

On George Babbitt's religion: Actually, the content of his theology was that there was a supreme being who had tried to make us perfect, but presumably had failed; that if one was a Good Man he would go to a place called Heaven (Babbitt unconsciously pictured it as rather like an excellent hotel with a private garden), but if one was a Bad Man, that is, if he murdered or committed burglary or used cocaine or had mistresses or sold non-existent real estate, he would be punished. Babbitt was uncertain, however, about what he called "this business of Hell." He explained to Ted, "Of course I'm pretty liberal; I don't exactly believe in a fire-and-brimstone Hell. Stands to reason, though, that a fellow can't get away with all sorts of Vice and not get nicked for it, see how I mean?"

CHAPTER 18 PART 1

Though he saw them twice daily, though he knew and amply discussed every detail of their expenditures, yet for weeks together Babbitt was no more conscious of his children than of the buttons on his coat-sleeves.

CHAPTER 18 PART 1

Babbitt was an average father. He was affectionate, bullying, opinionated, ignorant, and rather wistful. Like most parents, he enjoyed the game of waiting till the victim was clearly wrong, then virtuously pouncing.

CHAPTER 18 PART 5

Babbitt loved his mother, and sometimes he rather liked her.

Main Speak: Quotes from the Work of Sinclair Lewis

CHAPTER 22 PART 1

He wandered home and found his wife radiant with the horrified interest we have in the tragedies of our friends.

CHAPTER 23 PART 1

He was silent at dinner, unusually kindly to Ted and Verona, hesitating but not disapproving when Verona stated her opinion of Kenneth Escott's opinion of Dr. John Jennison Drew's opinion of the opinions of the evolutionists.

CHAPTER 27 PART 1

There was no one in Zenith who talked of anything but the strike, and no one who did not take sides. You were either a courageous friend of Labor, or you were a fearless supporter of the Rights of Property; and in either case you were belligerent, and ready to disown any friend who did not hate the enemy.

CHAPTER 29 PART 4

That evening Babbitt dined alone. He saw all the Clan of Good Fellows peering through the restaurant window, spying on him. Fear sat beside him, and he told himself that to-night he would not go to Tanis's flat; and he did not go...till late.

CHAPTER 34 PART 6

George Babbitt: "Now, for heaven's sake, don't repeat this to your mother, or she'd remove what little hair I've got left, but practically, I've never done a single thing I've wanted to in my whole life! I don't know's I've accomplished anything except just get along. I figure out I've made about a quarter of an inch out of a possible hundred rods. Well, maybe you'll carry things on further. I don't know. But I do get a kind of sneaking pleasure out of the fact that you knew what you wanted to do and did it. Well, those folks in there will try to bully you, and tame you down. Tell 'em to go to the devil!"

Michael Fridgen

Arrowsmith (1925)

Like *Babbitt*, *Arrowsmith* is another of Sinclair Lewis's titles
that should be more recognized. It is, quite possibly, the first
novel that portrays the culture of modern science. *Arrowsmith*
won the Pulitzer Prize in 1926; however, Lewis declined the
award. A few years earlier, in 1921, the Pulitzer committee
selected *Main Street* for the honor—but the Pulitzer Board of
Directors rejected *Main Street* because, they felt, it was far too
critical of America. Lewis could not handle the irony, as *Arrowsmith* is equally as critical, and he rejected the award.

Martin Arrowsmith is a frustrated medical doctor. He
desperately wants to be a researcher but often finds himself
encumbered with patients and other public officials. Today,
the medical community idolizes researchers and marginalizes doctors that treat aches, cancer, and depression. However,
back in Dr. Arrowsmith's time, researchers were seen as antisocial idiots, while a doctor whose only remedy was to go
home and move the bowels was considered a hero.

Sinclair Lewis's father was a small-town doctor in Sauk
Centre, Minnesota. He had an office on Main Street, but also a
small exam room at the family home. (Visitors to the Sinclair
Lewis boyhood home can see the exam room today.) Perhaps
there is part of Dr. Edwin Lewis in Dr. Martin Arrowsmith.

The amount of research that was required to write *Arrowsmith* is astounding. In a time well before television, the
complexity of science was reserved for a few select brains. In
order to write this novel, Lewis needed to infiltrate an exclusive culture that spoke and acted differently than ordinary
people. He enlisted the help of Paul de Kruif, an American microbiologist of the time. Paul de Kruif may have contributed

up to twenty-five percent of the book—and he went on to write his own mega-bestseller: *Microbe Hunters.*

Dr. Arrowsmith moves around a lot. The fictional town of Zenith is mentioned frequently, and the good doctor has lunch with one George F. Babbitt. And, in true Sinclair Lewis style, the relationships between husbands and wives are prominently featured.

Arrowsmith occurs at a time when science was not trusted. The communities featured in the novel don't understand Dr. Arrowsmith's work. They also highly resent being told how to live healthier lives. Politicians in Arrowsmith's world fight against him when science threatens to negatively impact the business community. (Does this sound familiar? We seem to be facing the same issues in 2020.)

Sometimes, while reading Lewis, I can't help but think that he must have had the ability to time travel. Interestingly, Sinclair Lewis was a huge fan of H.G. Wells and even named his first child Wells. Perhaps there is something to all this time travel stuff after all. Regardless, *Arrowsmith* is even more relevant today than it was in 1925.

CHAPTER 1 PART 2

There was a suspicion in Elk Mills-now, in 1897, a dowdy red-brick village, smelling of apples-that this brown-leather adjustable seat which Doc Vickerson used for minor operations, for the infrequent pulling of teeth and for highly frequent naps, had begun life as a barber's chair. There was also a belief that its proprietor must once have been called Doctor Vickerson, but for years he had been only The Doc, and he was scurfier and much less adjustable than the chair.

CHAPTER 2 PART 1

On the University of Winnemac: It is not a snobbish rich-man's college, devoted to leisurely nonsense. It is the property of the people of the state, and what they want-or what they are told they want-is a mill to turn out men and women who will lead moral lives, play bridge, drive good cars, be enterprising in business, and occasionally mention books, though they are not expected to have time to read them.

CHAPTER 2 PART 2

On Martin Arrowsmith's appeal: The co-eds murmured that he "looked so romantic," but as this was before the invention of sex and the era of petting-parties, they merely talked about him at a distance, and he did not know that he could have been a hero of amours.

CHAPTER 4 PART 1

On Professor Gottlieb inoculating a pig with anthrax during a lecture on bacteriology: The class was impatient. Why didn't he get on with it, on to the entertainingly dreadful moment of inoculating the pig? (And Max Gottlieb, glancing at the other guinea pig in the prison of its battery jar, meditated, "Wretched innocent! Why should I murder him, to teach Dummkopfe? It would be better to experiment on that fat young man.")

CHAPTER 4 PART 1

Gottlieb: "Gentlemen, the most important part of living is not the living but pondering upon it. And the most important part of experimentation is not doing the experiment but making notes, ve-ry accurate quantitative notes-in ink. I am told that a great many clever people feel they can keep notes in their heads. I have often observed with pleasure that such persons do not have heads in which to keep their notes. This is very good, because thus the world never sees their results and science is not encumbered with them."

CHAPTER 5 PART 2

It cannot be said, in this biography of a young man who was in no degree a hero, who regarded himself as a seeker after truth yet who stumbled and slid back all his life and bogged himself in every obvious morass, that Martin's intentions toward Madeline Fox were what is called "honorable." He was not a Don Juan, but he was a poor medical student who would have to wait for years before he could make a living. Certainly he did not think of proposing marriage. He wanted-like most poor and ardent young men in such a case, he wanted all he could get.

CHAPTER 5 PART 7

On Martin Arrowsmith and Madeline: They hurt each other; they had pleasure in it; and they parted forever, twice they parted forever, the second time very rudely, near a fraternity-house where students were singing heart-breaking summer songs to a banjo.

CHAPTER 6 PART 3

On Arrowsmith's first visit to the hospital as a medical student: He passed several nurses rapidly, half nodding to them, in the manner (or what he conceived to be the manner) of a brilliant young surgeon who is about to operate. He was so absorbed in looking like a brilliant young surgeon that he was completely lost, and discovered himself in a wing filled with private suites. He was late. He had no more time to go on being impressive. Like all males, he hated to confess ignorance by asking directions, but grudgingly he stopped at the door of a bedroom in which a probationer nurse was scrubbing the floor.

CHAPTER 7 PART 6

In the slightly Midwestern city of Zenith, the appearance of a play "with the original New York cast" was an event. (What Play it was did not much matter.)

CHAPTER 8 PART 2

Roscoe Geake on physicians as salespeople: "Nothing is more important in inspiring him than to have such an office that as soon as he steps into it, you have begun to sell him the idea of being properly cured. I don't care whether a doctor has studied in Germany, Munich, Baltimore, and Rochester. I don't care whether he has all science at his fingertips, whether he can instantly diagnose with a considerable degree of accuracy the most obscure ailment, whether he has the surgical technique of a Mayo, a Crile, a Blake, an Ochsner, a Cushing. If he has a dirty old office, with hand-me-down chairs and a lot of second-hand magazines, then the patient isn't going to have confidence in him; he is going to resist the treatment-and the doctor is going to have difficulty in putting over and collecting an adequate fee."

CHAPTER 9 PART 2

With each drink he admitted that he had an excellent chance to become a drunkard, and with each he boasted that he did not care.

CHAPTER 9 PART 2

Always, in America, there remains from pioneer days a cheerful pariahdom of shabby young men who prowl causelessly from state to state, from gang to gang, in the power of the Wanderlust. They wear black sateen shirts, and carry bundles. They are not permanently tramps. They have home towns to which they return, to work quietly in the factory or the section-gang for a year-for a week-and as quietly to disappear again. They crowd the smoking cars at night; they sit silent on benches in filthy stations; they know all the land yet of it they know nothing, because in a hundred cities they see only the employment agencies, the all-night lunches, the blind-pigs, the scabrous lodging-houses.

CHAPTER 11 PART 2

The Doctor, and The Doctor alone, was safe by night in the slum called "the Arbor." His black bag was a pass. Policemen saluted him, prostitutes bowed to him without mockery, saloon-keepers called out, "Evenin', Doc," and hold-up men stood back in doorways to let him pass. Martin had power, the first obvious power in his life. And he was led into incessant adventure. He took a bank-president out of a dive; he helped the family conceal the disgrace; he irritably refused their bribe; and afterward, when he thought of how he might have dined with Leora, he was sorry he had refused it. He broke into hotel-rooms reeking with gas and revived would-be suicides. He drank Trinidad rum with a Congressman who advocated prohibition. He attended a policeman assaulted by strikers, and a striker assaulted by policemen.

CHAPTER 13 PART 2

Gottlieb, the placidly virulent hater of religious rites, had a religious-seeming custom. Often he knelt by his bed and let his mind run free. It was very much like prayer, though certainly there was no formal invocation, no consciousness of a Supreme Being-other than Max Gottlieb.

CHAPTER 15 PART 3

Martin became the demon driver of the village. To ride with him was to sit holding your hat, your eyes closed, waiting for death. Apparently he accelerated for corners, to make them more interesting. The sight of anything on the road ahead, from another motor to a yellow pup, stirred in him a frenzy which could be stilled only by going up and passing it. The village adored, "The Young Doc is quite some driver, all right." They waited, with amiable interest, to hear that he had been killed.

CHAPTER 15 PART 5

Unnamed farmer: "Yoost keep to the right. You can't miss it." Probably no one who has listened to the dire "you can't miss it" has ever failed to miss it.

CHAPTER 16 PART 3

He told himself that these villagers were generous; that their snooping was in part an affectionate interest, and inevitable in a village where the most absorbing event of the year was the United Brethren Sunday School picnic on Fourth of July. But he could not rid himself of twitchy discomfort at their unending and maddeningly detailed comments on everything. He felt as though the lightest word he said in his consultation-room would be megaphoned from flapping ear to ear all down the country roads.

CHAPTER 16 PART 5

On Arrowsmith's view of childbirth: He denounced Nature for her way of tricking human beings, by every gay device of moonlight and white limbs and reaching loneliness, into having babies, then making birth as cruel and clumsy and wasteful as she could.

Michael Fridgen

CHAPTER 17 PART 1

Dr. Coughlin: "Great mistake for any doctor to not identify himself with some good solid religious denomination, whether he believes the stuff or not. I tell you a priest or a preacher can send you an awful lot of business."

CHAPTER 17 PART 5

Dr. Sondelius: "The medical profession can have but one desire: to destroy the medical profession. As for the laymen, they can be sure of but one thing: nine-tenths of what they know about health is not so, and with the other tenth they do nothing."

CHAPTER 18 PART 1

When the neighborhood suddenly achieved a real epidemic of diphtheria and Martin shakily preached antitoxin, one-half of them remembered his failure to save Mary Novak and the other half clamored, "Oh, give us a rest! You got epidemics on the brain!" That a number of children quite adequately died did not make them relinquish their comic epic.

CHAPTER 19 PART 1

Nautilus is to Zenith what Zenith is to Chicago. With seventy thousand people, it is a smaller Zenith but no less brisk. There is one large hotel to compare with the dozen in Zenith, but that one is as busy and standardized and frenziedly modern as its owner can make it. The only authentic difference between Nautilus and Zenith is that in both cases all the streets look alike but in Nautilus they do not look alike for so many miles. The difficulty in defining its quality is that no one has determined whether it is a very large village or a very small city.

CHAPTER 19 PART 4

Martin had to take the twins on his knees and tell them a story. They were remarkably heavy twins, but no heavier than the labor of inventing a plot.

CHAPTER 20 PART 1

It is one of the major tragedies that nothing is more discomforting than the hearty affection of the Old Friends who never were friends.

CHAPTER 21 PART 1

Nautilus was one of the first communities in the country to develop the Weeks habit, now so richly grown that we have Correspondence School Week, Christian Science Week, Osteopathy Week, and Georgia Pine Week. A Week is not merely a week. If an aggressive, wide-awake, live-wire, and go-ahead church or chamber of commerce or charity desires to improve itself, which means to get more money, it calls in those few energetic spirits who run any city, and proclaims a Week. This consists of one month of committee meetings, a hundred columns of praise for the organization in the public prints, and finally a day or two on which athletic persons flatter unappreciative audiences in churches or cinema theaters, and the prettiest girls in town have the pleasure of being allowed to talk to male strangers on the street corners, apropos of giving them extremely undecorative tags in exchange for the smallest sums which those strangers think they must pay if they are to be considered gentlemen.

CHAPTER 23 PART 1

The Health Fair opened with crowds and success. There was a slight misunderstanding the first day. The Master Bakers' Association spoke strongly to Pickerbaugh about the sign "Too much pie makes pyorrhea" on the diet booth. But the thoughtless and prosperity-destroying sign was removed at once, and the Fair was thereafter advertised in every bakery in town.

CHAPTER 23 PART 4

On Martin Arrowsmith replacing Pickerbaugh: The train moved out, Pickerbaugh waving as long as he could see them. And Martin to Leora, "Oh, he's a fine old boy. He-No, I'm hanged if he is! The world's always letting people get away with asininities because they're kind-hearted. And here I've sat back like a coward, not saying a word, and watched 'em loose that wind-storm on the whole country. Oh, curse it, isn't anything in the world simple? Well, let's go to the office, and I'll begin to do things conscientiously and all wrong."

CHAPTER 25 PART 1

On Arrowsmith's Philosophy of truth and work: He insisted that there is no Truth but only many truths; that Truth is not a colored bird to be chased among the rocks and captured by its tail, but a skeptical attitude toward life. He insisted that no one could expect more than, by stubbornness or luck, to have the kind of work he enjoyed and an ability to become better acquainted with the facts of that work than the average job-holder.

CHAPTER 26 PART 1

Dr. Gottlieb: "Succeed? I have heard that word. It is English? Oh, yes, it is a word that liddle schoolboys use at the University of Winnemac. It means passing examinations. But there are no examinations to pass here. Martin, let us be clear. You know something of laboratory technique; you have heard about dese bacilli; you are not a good chemist, and mathematics-pfui!-most terrible! But you have curiosity and you are stubborn. You do not accept rules. Therefore I t'ink you will either make a very good scientist or a very bad one, and if you are bad enough, you will be popular with the rich ladies who rule this city, New York, and you can gif lectures for a living or even become, if you get to be plausible enough, a college president. So anyvay, it will be interesting."

CHAPTER 26 PART 1

Dr. Gottlieb: "To be a scientist-it is not just a different job, so that a man should choose between being a scientist and being an explorer or a bond-salesman or a physician or a king or a farmer. It is a tangle of ver-y obscure emotions, like mysticism, or wanting to write poetry; it makes its victim all different from the good normal man. The normal man, he does not care much what he does except that he should eat and sleep and make love. But the scientist is intensely religious-he is so religious that he will not accept quarter-truths, because they are an insult to his faith. He wants that everything should be subject to inexorable laws. He is equal opposed to the capitalists who t'ink their silly money-grabbing is a system, and to liberals who t'ink man is not a fighting animal; he takes both the American booster and the European aristocrat, and he ignores all their blithering. Ignores it! All of it! He hates the preachers who talk their fables, but he is not too kindly to the anthropologists and historians who can only make guesses, yet they have the nerf to call themselves scientists! Oh, yes, he is a man that all nice good-natured people should naturally hate!"

CHAPTER 26 PART 1

Dr. Martin Arrowsmith: "God give me unclouded eyes and freedom from haste. God give me a quiet and relentless anger against all pretense and all pretentious work and all work left slack and unfinished. God give me a restlessness whereby I may neither sleep nor accept praise till my observed results equal my calculated results or in pious glee I discover and assault my error. God give me strength not to trust to God!"

CHAPTER 27 PART 1

With all his amateurish fumbling, Martin had one characteristic without which there can be no science: a wide-ranging, sniffing, snuffling, undignified, unself-dramatizing curiosity, and it drove him on.

CHAPTER 27 PART 6

Terry Wickett on his enlistment into World War One: "I'm ashamed of chucking my work like this, and I certainly don't want to kill Germans-I mean not any more'n I want to kill most people-but I never could resist getting into a big show."

CHAPTER 27 PART 6

Dr. Arrowsmith on World War One: "Mind you, I'm anti-German all right-I think they're probably just as bad as we are."

CHAPTER 27 PART 8

It was Martin's most pitiful fault that he was not very kind to shy people and lonely people and stupid old people; he was not cruel to them, he simply was unconscious of them or so impatient of their fumbling that he avoided them. "Very few people have the courage to be decently selfish-not answer letters–and demand the right to work. If they had their way, these sentimentalists would've had a Newton-yes, or probably a Christ!-giving up everything they did for the world to address meetings and listen to the troubles of cranky old maids. Nothing takes so much courage as to keep hard and clear-headed."

CHAPTER 28 PART 1

Through the film Martin gave his opinion, as a captain and as a doctor, that it seemed improbable a mother should not know her daughter after an absence of ten years. He was restless and rational, which is not a mood in which to view the cinema.

CHAPTER 34 PART 4

Dr. Sondelius: "Gottlieb is right about these jests of God. Yey! His best one is the tropics. God planned them so beautiful, flowers and sea and mountains. He made the fruit to grow so well that man need not work-and then He laughed, and stuck in volcanoes and snakes and damp heat and early senility and the plague and malaria. But the nastiest trick He ever played on man was inventing the flea."

CHAPTER 37 PART 5

On Martin and Joyce's trip to Europe: They really had, it seemed, to stay with the Principessa del Oltraggio (formerly Miss Lucy Dee-my Bessy of Dayton), Madame des Basses Loges (Miss Brown of San Francisco), and the Countess of Marazion (who had been Mrs. Arthur Snaipe of Albany, and several things before that), but Joyce did go with him to see the great laboratories in London, Paris, Copenhagen.

CHAPTER 39 PART 1

Martin and Clif settled in large chairs in the drawing-room, and tried to play at being old friends happy in meeting. They did not look at each other.

CHAPTER 40 PART 1

Joyce: "Martin, do you need to emphasize your arguments by a 'by God' in every sentence, or have you a few other expressions in your highly scientific vocabulary?"

Mantrap (1926)

If Sinclair Lewis and Jack London had a child together, that child would be *Mantrap*. It's not that odd of a proposition, because the two did know each other. In 1910, Sinclair Lewis left Yale during the middle of his education. He wanted to ascertain whether he really needed to complete a degree in order to make it as a writer. After giving up on a few newspaper jobs he landed in California where a Yale classmate offered him a minimal position with a publishing house. There, he met Jack London.

London was going through a bit of a tough time. He was suffering through a particularly bad case of writer's block and the vultures were starting to circle. He was close to losing his ranch to creditors and was completely out of ideas. Sinclair Lewis was also in need of money. He had decided that he wanted to return to Yale and complete his degree; however, he did not have the funds to travel across the county. Sinclair's father, Dr. Lewis, refused to give him any more money. (Dr. Lewis and his wife were certainly not the helicopter parents of today–a fact that Sinclair Lewis came to appreciate greatly in his adult years.)

Sinclair Lewis always carried with him several notebooks where he could jot plot ideas as they came to him. He was also a prolific collector of names to use for characters, most of these he wrote down as he walked through cemeteries. Jack London offered to purchase some of Lewis's plot ideas and character names. It's not known how much Sinclair Lewis inspiration ended up in a Jack London novel, but it's quite probable that London wrote at least two complete books from Lewis's ideas.

Regardless, London got a little tonic for his writer's block, and Lewis got enough money to return to Yale.

The first quarter and last quarter of *Mantrap* are reminiscent of a Jack London wilderness adventure tale. The middle is pure Sinclair Lewis relationship trauma. There isn't any satire in *Mantrap*, and it probably won't change anyone's life after having read it. Still, it's a good read for a road trip.

Mantrap tells the story of Ralph Prescott, New York City attorney, and his journey through the northern woods of Canada. He endures many typical trials and tribulations, then, unexpectedly, gets himself mixed-up with a married couple along the banks of the Mantrap River. Lewis was quite purposeful in his choice to name the river 'Mantrap.'

Ralph begins an unusual friendship with a man named Joe Easter, so let's talk about the pink elephant in the room: homosexuality. There's nothing ever specifically mentioned in any of Lewis's works; however, several of his books include unique male relationships. Today, we would call these relationships "bromances." I believe that Sinclair Lewis was trying to tell us something about himself. Either he understood homosexuality in a more personal way than we can know, or, perhaps he yearned for a deep and meaningful friendship that was missing from his life. Regardless, Lewis was born in 1885 and we can only speculate about what was going on inside his body. Even if he did have a greater understanding of sexual differences, he would still be very reticent to express any of that understanding overtly–everyone was homophobic in 1885, even the homosexuals.

Mantrap was originally published as a serial in *Collier's* magazine. A silent black-and-white film, also called *Mantrap*, was released shortly after the collection of serial articles was assembled into a novel.

Main Speak: Quotes from the Work of Sinclair Lewis

CHAPTER 1

At forty Ralph Prescott was more than ever a bachelor. The explanation was a mother so much more serene and fine and instantly understanding than any girl he encountered that he had preferred her dear presence to insinuating romance. But she had been dead these two years, and where she had once coaxed him away from his desk at midnight for a chat and easy laughter and a glass of milk before she ordered him off to bed, he sought now to fill the vacuum of her absence by working till one–till two–till weary dawn.

CHAPTER 2

Tents, blankets, canoes, and the like had been arranged for by Woodbury's friend in Winnipeg, and would be awaiting them at railhead, at Whitewater, so Ralph contented himself with not more than two or three times as many things as he needed.

CHAPTER 3

Ralph Prescott: "Am I going to be afraid all the while?" he agonized. His joy in adventure had dimmed; it almost vanished as he listened to the chatter, as he heard of wolves, of forest fires, of canoes capsized while sailing on lakes ten miles wide, of canoes sinking in a storm when they struck hidden snags. And with his dreary apprehensions was a certain boredom.

CHAPTER 3

Thus afraid of being afraid, which is of all fears the most unmanning and pitiful, Ralph sat paralyzed; and hour by tedious hour, as they crept through the dusty jack pines, as the train stopped at every lone wheat-elevator, and switched box-cars for interminable vacuities, his torpor was broken only by irritation at Woodbury's manly laughter.

(Note: Sinclair Lewis wrote *Thus afraid of being afraid, which is of all fears the most unmanning and pitiful*, fifteen years before Franklin Delano Roosevelt paraphrased the sentiment.)

CHAPTER 4

Ralph Prescott had been brought up on the Fenimore Cooper tradition of Indians. He expected all of them to look like the chieftain on the buffalo nickel, like the statue which in all proper parks stands between Goethe in marble and General Sherman in bronze—a sachem eagle-nosed, tall, magnificently grave. His heart was pinched as he saw shambling toward them four swart and runty loafers, introduced as Jesse, Louey, Charley, and Nick.

(Note: Fenimore Cooper was a writer of historical fiction born in 1789. He is best known for *The Last of the Mohicans.*)

CHAPTER 7

On Mr. Wesson Woodbury's demeanor: He went on with as much joy in hurting his companion and hurting himself, and hurling out nastiness which he would later regret, as though he were a drunkard accused of being a drunkard.

CHAPTER 10

On Ralph Prescott meeting Mrs. Alverna Easter for the first time: Ralph Prescott, the professional bachelor, was in fact considerably more excited about the presence of Alverna than he had been about fifteen-point muskalonge, the prospect of seeing a moose, E. Wesson Woodbury's travail with the outboard motor, or anything he had experienced in the wild Northland save the sturdy friendship of Joe Easter.

CHAPTER 12

They were his family, he felt grimly; for Joe or Alverna he would zealously cut the throat of Mrs. McGavity, and that would be no brief task nor pretty.

CHAPTER 12

Joe Easter: "I don't like being murdered more'n most folks, in my bed or anywhere else."

CHAPTER 13

Ralph had tried to drink as little as possible. Certainly, in any investigation of the affair, it is known that he had always hated drunkenness as he hated split infinitives or the devil or white-edged black dinner-ties.

CHAPTER 17

Alverna Easter: "Oh, Ralph, I was so bored here! I didn't think anything *could* be worse than being so bored. But there is: being so scared. I'm just never myself. I'm always waiting for something dreadful to happen. And I don't know from which way it might be coming. Oh—*terrified!*"

CHAPTER 18

Alverna Easter: "I wonder if there ever was a man of honor who had so much honor that he could sacrifice it for a woman?"

CHAPTER 21

On Joe believing that Ralph and Alverna have had an indiscretion: He glanced from Ralph to Alverna. They must have looked too expressionlessly innocent for innocence.

Michael Fridgen

Elmer Gantry (1927)

Elmer Gantry is one of those rare novels that I can pick up, read any random Chapter, and put it down having discovered something new about us humans. Even though the complete story is riveting, it's clear that Lewis constructed each Chapter to convey a particular aspect of religion. Each Chapter can, for the most part, stand alone.

Fans of the famous film version of *Elmer Gantry* should know that there is much more to the story. The film mainly focuses on one section of the novel. Also, once again, the city of Zenith plays an important role in this book. (George Babbitt himself makes a cameo appearance). However, Elmer's Zenith is a whole other entity compared with Babbitt's Zenith. (Elmer's Zenith lies either above or below Babbitt's Zenith–depending upon the reader's perspective.)

What a character Elmer Gantry is! I'm so repulsed by this man that I can hardly think of his name without shaking my head. At the same time, I know that I would absolutely welcome him into my life if I had the chance. I would love the authenticity we'd have as he would confide his true nature to me. And, I would be envious of his ability to turn his inauthenticity with others into millions of dollars.

Sinclair Lewis is less gray about Elmer Gantry than he is with Carol Kennicott and George Babbitt. Elmer Gantry is written to be evil. The only redeeming quality of his entire existence is a spark of affection toward Sharon Falconer. But if Elmer is so vile, why do so many allow themselves to be taken in by him? On Facebook, my relationship with *Elmer Gantry* would be: It's complicated.

Gantry, the man, is like that old great-uncle who nobody can stand. He's opinionated, rude, and self-righteous. However, he knows the exact compliment to give at the exact right time—and we love him for this small morsel of humanity. Yes, he's a sociopath, and we should not fall for it. But we do.

Unfortunately, there is one famous quote of the Reverend Elmer Gantry that I have not listed here. Whenever Gantry is called upon to preach to a congregation for the first time, he recites an early and quite successful sermon. Initially, he crafted this sermon by pure accident and luck. However, it turns out to be so effective at saving souls that he uses it frequently throughout his career. The sermon is about love; it compares love to the morning star and the evening star...and a bunch of other things. I omitted quotes from this particular sermon because Sinclair Lewis intended readers to encounter its message numerous times during the life of Elmer Gantry—it's not my prerogative to deprive anyone of the joy of discovering the good reverend's repetitive banter.

It's almost a crime that librarians all over the globe shelve *Elmer Gantry* with the fiction. In my estimation, it's about as non-fiction as any work of literature could possibly be. If you doubt this assertion, just pick up a current newspaper or read any news source online. The themes of *Elmer Gantry* are found right in the headlines of any story about the state of modern American politics.

CHAPTER 1 PART 1
He was born to be a senator. He never said anything important, and he always said it sonorously.

CHAPTER 1 PART 1
The light was dim, completely soothing, coming through fantastic windows such as are found only in churches, saloons, jewelry shops, and other retreats from reality.

Michael Fridgen

CHAPTER 1 PART 6

On Elmer Gantry's early feeling toward religion: The church, full thirty dizzy feet up to its curiously carven rafters, and the preachers, so overwhelming in their wallowing voices, so terrifying in their pictures of little boys who stole watermelons or indulged in biological experiments behind barns. The awe-oppressed moment of his second conversion, at the age of eleven, when, weeping with embarrassment and the prospect of losing so much fun, surrounded by solemn and whiskered adult faces, he had signed a pledge binding him to give up, forever, the joys of profanity, alcohol, cards, dancing, and the theater.

CHAPTER 2 PART 1

On the bare floor of Eddie's room, over Knute Halvorsted's paint-shop, from three to sixteen young men knelt at a time, and no 1800 revival saw more successful wrestling with the harassed Satan. In fact one man, suspected of Holy Roller sympathies, managed to have the jerks, and while they felt that this was carrying things farther than the Lord and the Baptist association would care to see it, added excitement to praying at three o'clock in the morning, particularly as they were all of them extraordinarily drunk on coffee and eloquence.

CHAPTER 2 PART 2

Whatever difficulties he may have had with philosophy, Latin, and calculus, there had never been a time since the age of twelve when Eddie Fislinger had had difficulty in understanding what the Lord God Almighty wanted, and why, all through history, he had acted thus or thus.

CHAPTER 3 PART 3

On Elmer Gantry's mother: She was weeping, old eyes puckered, and in her weeping was his every recollection of winter dawns when she had let him stay in bed and brought porridge to him across the icy floor; winter evenings when he had awakened to find her still stitching; and that confusing intimidating hour, in the abyss of his first memories, when he had seen her shaken beside a coffin that contained a cold monster in the shape of his father.

Main Speak: Quotes from the Work of Sinclair Lewis

CHAPTER 3 PART 7

Judson Roberts on his own preaching: "No, really, it wasn't so bad for him, that Elmer what's-his-name, to get converted. Suppose there isn't anything to it. Won't hurt him to cut out some of his bad habits for a while, anyway. And how do we know? Maybe the Holy Ghost does come down. No more improbable than electricity. I do wish I could get over this doubting! I forget it when I've got 'em going in an evangelistic meeting, but when I watch a big butcher like him, with that damn' silly smirk on his jowls—I believe I'll go into the real estate business. I don't think I'm hurting these young fellows any, but I do wish I could be honest. Oh, Lordy, Lordy, Lordy, I wish I had a good job selling real estate!"

CHAPTER 4 PART 1

The only things he had against the ministry, now that he was delivered from Jim, were the low salaries and the fact that if ministers were caught drinking or flirting, it was often very hard on them. The salaries weren't so bad—he'd go to the top, of course, and maybe make eight or ten thousand. But the diversions—He thought about it so much that he made a hasty trip to Cato, and came back temporarily cured forever of any desire for wickedness.

CHAPTER 4 PART 2

Dr. Quarles: "Brother Elmer, the last thing I'd ever want to do, in fairness to the spirit of the ministry, would be to create an illusion of a Call when there was none present. That would be like the pagan hallucinations worked on the poor suffering followers of Roman Catholicism. Whatever else he may be, a Baptist preacher must be free from illusions; he must found his work on good hard scientific facts—the proven facts of the Bible, and substitutionary atonement, which even pragmatically we know to be true, because it works."

CHAPTER 5 PART 1

He had an elegant vocabulary. He knew eighteen synonyms for sin, half of them very long and impressive, and the others very short and explosive and minatory—minatory being one of his own best words, constantly useful in terrifying the as yet imaginary horde of sinners gathered before him.

CHAPTER 6 PART 1

There is a Northern and Southern convention of this distinguished denomination, because before the Civil War the Northern Baptists proved by the Bible, unanswerably, that slavery was wrong; and the Southern Baptists proved by the Bible, irrefutably, that slavery was the will of God.

CHAPTER 7 PART 2

However, for the benefit of the more leathery and zealous deacons down front, he permitted them to hate all Catholics, all persons who failed to believe in hell and immersion, and all rich mortgage-holders, wantoning in the betraying smiles of scarlet women, each of whom wore silk and in her bejeweled hand held a ruby glass of perfidious wine.

CHAPTER 8 PART 2

But both imagination and reason had been submerged in a religion in which doubt was not only sinful but, much worse, in bad taste.

CHAPTER 8 PART 2

Frank Shallard: "But you wouldn't want it destroyed? Even if some details of dogma aren't true—or even all of 'em—think what a consolation religion and the church are to weak humanity!"

Dr. Zechlin: "Are they? I wonder! Don't cheerful agnostics, who know they're going to die dead, worry much less than good Baptists, who worry lest their sons and cousins and sweethearts fail to get into the Baptist heaven—or what is even worse, who wonder if they may not have guessed wrong—if God may not be a Catholic, maybe, or a Mormon or a Seventh-day Adventist instead of a Baptist, and then they'll go to hell themselves! Consolation? No!"

CHAPTER 8 PART 5

Elmer Gantry never knew who sent him thirty dimes, wrapped in a tract about holiness, nor why. But he found the sentiments in the tract useful in a sermon, and the thirty dimes he spent for lively photographs of burlesque ladies.

CHAPTER 10 PART 3

Elmer Gantry: "Sure; preachers can cuss and make love just like anybody else. I know! What they get away with, pretending to be different," said Elmer lugubriously, "would make you gentlemen tired if you knew."

CHAPTER 12 PART 1

Sharon Falconer: "Damn it, Elmer, don't say 'damn it'! Oh, I hate the little vices—smoking, swearing, scandal, drinking just enough to be silly. I love the big ones—murder, lust, cruelty, ambition!"

CHAPTER 13 PART 2

The churches were suspicious of women evangelists—women might do very well in visiting the sick, knitting for the heathen, and giving strawberry festivals, but they couldn't shout loud enough to scare the devil out of sinners. Indeed all evangelists, men and women, were under attack. Sound churchmen here and there were asking whether there was any peculiar spiritual value in frightening people into groveling maniacs.

CHAPTER 13 PART 5

In Scranton, they had unusually exasperating patients. Scranton had been saved by a number of other evangelists before their arrival, and had become almost anesthetic. Ten nights they sweated over the audience without a single sinner coming forward, and Elmer had to go out and hire half a dozen convincing converts. He found them in a mission near the river, and explained that by giving a good example to the slothful, they would be doing the work of God, and that if the example was good enough, he would give them five dollars apiece. The missioner himself came in during the conference and offered to get converted for ten, but he was so well known that Elmer had to give him the ten to stay away.

CHAPTER 15 PART 1

Healing was later to become the chief feature of many evangelists, but in 1910 it was advertised chiefly by Christian Scientists and the New Thoughters. Sharon came to it by accident. She had regularly offered prayers for the sick, but only absent-mindedly. When Elmer and she had been together for a year, during her meetings in Schenectady a man led up his deaf wife and begged Sharon to heal her. It amused Sharon to send out for some oil (it happened to be shotgun oil, but she properly consecrated it) to anoint the woman's ears, and to pray lustily for healing.

CHAPTER 16 PART 1

On Mrs. Evans Riddle: She instructed small Select Circles how to keep one's husband, how to understand Sanskrit philosophy without understanding either Sanskrit or philosophy, and how to become slim without giving up pastry. She healed all the diseases in the medical dictionary, and some which were not; and in personal consultations, at ten dollars the half hour, she explained to unappetizing elderly ladies how they might rouse passion in a football hero.

CHAPTER 16 PART 2

In some ways he preferred New Thought to standard Protestantism. It was safer to play with. He had never been sure but that there might be something to the doctrines he had preached as an evangelist. Perhaps God really had dictated every word of the Bible. Perhaps there really was a hell of burning sulphur. Perhaps the Holy Ghost really was hovering around watching him and reporting. But he knew with serenity that all of his New Thoughts, his theosophical utterances, were pure and uncontaminated bunk. No one could deny his theories because none of his theories meant anything.

CHAPTER 17 PART 1

So Frank Shallard, pupil of Bruno Zechlin, said nervously to an examining cleric that, yes, he did believe that baptism by immersion was appointed by God himself, as the only valid way of beginning a righteous life; that, yes, unrepentant sinners would go to a literal Hell; that, yes, these unrepentant sinners included all persons who did not go to evangelical churches if they had the chance; and that, yes, the Maker of a universe with stars a hundred thousand light-years apart was interested, furious, and very personal about it if a small boy played baseball on Sunday afternoon.

CHAPTER 18 PART 1

Elmer Gantry: "That's the stunt! I'm sick of playing this lone game. Get in with a real big machine like the Methodists–maybe have to start low down, but climb fast–be a bishop myself in ten years–with all their spondulix and big churches and big membership and everything to back me up. Me for it. O Lord, thou hast guided me…No, honest, I mean it…No more hell-raising. Real religion from now on. Hurray!"

CHAPTER 18 PART 5

Fortunately, except in a few fashionable churches, it wasn't necessary to say anything original to succeed among the Baptists or Methodists.

CHAPTER 19 PART 3

He knew that she was the sort of wife who would help him to capture a bishopric. He persuaded himself that, with all her virtue, she would eventually be interesting to kiss.

CHAPTER 20 PART 6

In his attention to business, Elmer had not given especial heed to the collections. It had not been carelessness, for he knew his technique as a Professional Good Man. But the first day, he felt, he ought to establish himself as a spiritual leader, and when they all understood that, he would see to it that they paid suitably for the spiritual leadership. Was not the Laborer worthy of his Hire?

CHAPTER 23 PART 2

Though there were nearly four hundred thousand people in Zenith and only nine hundred in Banjo Crossing, Elmer's reception in the Zenith church-basement was remarkably like his reception in the Banjo basement. There were the same rugged, hard-handed brothers, the same ample sisters renowned for making doughnuts, the same brisk little men given to giggling and pious jests. There were the same homemade ice cream and homemade oratory.

CHAPTER 23 PART 5
In response to every sermon he had messages informing him that he was the bright hope of evangelicism and that he was a cloven-hoofed fiend; that he was a rousing orator and a human saxophone.

CHAPTER 25 PART 1
Elmer had, even in Zenith, to meet plenty of solemn and whiskery persons whose only pleasure aside from not doing agreeable things was keeping others from doing them. But the general bleakness of his sect was changing, and he found in Wellspring Church a Young Married Set who were nearly as cheerful as though they did not belong to a church.

CHAPTER 26 PART 2
He had made one discovery superb in its simple genius—the best way to get money was to ask for it, hard enough and often enough. To call on rich men, to set Sunday School classes in competition against one another, to see that every one received pledge-envelopes, these were all useful and he pursued them earnestly.

CHAPTER 26 PART 3
Father Smeesby: "My church, gentlemen, probably has a more rigid theology than yours, but I don't think we're quite so alarmed by discovering the fact, which seems to astonish you, that sinners often sin. The Catholic Church may be harder to believe, but it's easier to live with."

CHAPTER 28
Frank Shallard: "And," went on Frank, "tomorrow I've got a funeral. That Henry Semp. Weighed two hundred and eighty pounds from the neck down and three ounces from the neck up. Perfectly good Christian citizen who believed that Warren G. Harding was the greatest

man since George Washington. I'm sure he never beat his wife. Worthy communicant. But when his wife came to hire me, she wept like the dickens when she talked about Henry's death, but I noticed from the window that when she went off down the street she looked particularly cheerful. Yes, Henry was a bulwark of the nation; not to be sneered at by highbrows. And I'm dead certain, from something she said, that every year they've jipped the Government out of every cent they could on their income tax. And tomorrow I'm supposed to stand up there and tell his friends what a moral example and intellectual Titan he was, and how the poor little woman is simply broken by sorrow. Well, cheer up! From what I know of her, she'll be married again within six months, and if I do a good job of priesting tomorrow, maybe I'll get the fee! Oh, Lord, Phil, what a job, what a lying compromising job, this being a minister!"

CHAPTER 28

Philip McGarry to Frank Shallard: "I know that if you could lose your intellectual pride, if you could forget that you have to make a new world, better'n the Creator's, right away tonight–you and Bernard Shaw and H. G. Wells and H. L. Mencken and Sinclair Lewis (Lord, how that book of Lewis', 'Main Street,' did bore me, as much of it as I read; it just rambled on forever, and all he could see was that some of the Gopher Prairie hicks didn't go to literary teas quite as often as he does!–that was all he could see among those splendid heroic pioneers)!"

CHAPTER 28

Frank Shallard: "Just what are the teachings of Christ? Did he come to bring peace or more war? He says both. Did he approve earthly monarchies or rebel against them? He says both. Did he ever–think of it, God himself, taking on human form to help the earth–did he ever suggest sanitation, which would have saved millions from plagues? And you can't say his failure there was because he was too lofty to consider mere sickness. On the contrary, he was awfully interested in it, always healing some one–providing they flattered his vanity enough! There's just one thing that does stand out clearly and uncontradicted in Jesus' teaching. He advocated a system of economics whereby no one saved money or stored up wheat or did anything but live like a tramp. If this teaching of his had been accepted, the world would have starved in twenty years, after his death!"

(Note: Chapter 28 of *Elmer Gantry* is a section of the novel that stands alone; it does little to advance the story and is the only Chapter in the book not divided into parts. This Chapter brilliantly serves to present Sinclair Lewis's own theology in the voice of Frank Shallard. I've found that Chapter 28 is worth whatever the reader paid for the entire novel.)

CHAPTER 29 PART 7

Frank Shallard: "I had refused to resign. I still feel I have an honest right to an honest pulpit. But I am setting brother against brother. I am not a Cause—I am only a friend. I have loved you and the work, the sound of friends singing together, the happiness of meeting on leisurely Sunday mornings. This I give up. I resign, and I wish I could say, 'God be with you and bless you all.' But the good Christians have taken God and made him into a menacing bully, and I cannot even say 'God bless you,' during this last moment, in a life given altogether to religion, when I shall ever stand in a pulpit."

The Man Who Knew Coolidge: Being the Soul of Lowell Schmaltz, Constructive and Nordic Citizen (1928)

The Man Who Knew Coolidge is a quite different sort of work. While it is completely satirical, there is no plot. The entire book is a collection of monologues delivered by one Lowell Schmaltz. This novel, depending upon the reader's perspective, is either incredibly funny or incredibly sad. It cannot be both. Since I've had the unfortunate experience of knowing a few Lowell Schmaltz's, and consequently, since I have the knowledge that Lowell Schmaltz's do really exist, I find the book incredibly sad.

Lowell Schmaltz is exactly like his name sounds. While he has talked *to* a great many people in his life, he has never spoken *with* any of them. It's fitting that the book is comprised of his monologues, because it's likely Lowell never had a dialog in his life–he talks entirely too much to listen.

Schmaltz lives in Zenith, Winnemac and is, pretty much, an authority on everything. He has also traveled extensively (he claims), and he went to college with the man who would be President Coolidge (however, it's debatable whether he ever met him). From the monologues, we also learn that he's married with two adult children, sells office products for a living, is having financial difficulties, and quite possibly has ADHD. (His exact diagnosis is unknown, although my psychiatrist husband says that Schmaltz has an advanced form of the personality disorder officially known as 'Asshole Syndrome.' Regardless, Lowell Schmaltz needs medication–fast.)

The first monologue is given by Lowell inside a Pullman car on a moving train. He is speaking to a bunch of men, regaling them with the story of how he went (or rather, attempted to go) to the White House to see his old friend Calvin Coolidge. The second monologue is delivered as Lowell Schmaltz is playing cards in a hotel room. During this monologue he is trying to tell an anti-Semitic joke but never gets to the punch line. The third monologue finds Mr. Schmaltz attempting to get a loan from his cousin Walt.

When Schmalz returns to Zenith after seeing Walt, he presents the fourth monologue to his wife, Mame. The fifth monologue is a one-sided conversation over a plate of fried chicken at the home of Mr. and Mrs. Babbitt. Not even George Babbitt can get a word in edgewise when Lowell is on a roll. (Come to think of it, how does Lowell ever eat? Seriously, with the way his mouth moves, he must be the skinniest person in Zenith.)

The last monologue is delivered to the Men's Club of the Zenith Pilgrim Congregational Church. In attendance, and all the way from New York City, is none other than the Reverend Elmer Gantry. While it's quite nice not to have to endure Gantry's morning and evening star routine, Lowell Schmaltz manages to, once again, say a lot without saying much of anything.

This is pretty much the point of the novel. It's a portrait of a man who lacks any level of self-awareness. Lowell must be extremely insecure. The incessant bantering is, most likely, a device to cover for a lack of any real substance. It's a learned behavior—and that's why I find *The Man Who Knew Coolidge* so depressing to read.

Do not get the idea that Lowell's monologues in any way represent the voice of Sinclair Lewis. This work is entirely satirical, mostly because it's clear that Lewis absolutely despises Lowell Schmaltz. Also, while reading *The Man Who Knew Coolidge*, read every footnote and editor's comment. They are hysterical and prove that Sinclair Lewis would have been the lead writer for *The Simpsons* had he been born in a later century.

Main Speak: Quotes from the Work of Sinclair Lewis

(Editor's Note: Since the book consists of monologues, all selections below are attributed to Mr. Lowell Schmaltz.)

PART ONE: THE MAN WHO KNEW COOLIDGE

"What I say about prohibition is: Once a law has been passed by the duly elected and qualified representatives of the people of these United States, in fact once it's on the statue books, it's *there*, and it's there to be enforced. There hadn't ought to be any blind pigs or illegal stills. But the same time, that don't mean you got to be a fanatic."

On Queen Marie of Bulgaria: "By the way, Queen Marie made quite a stay at Zenith. She stopped over pretty near an hour between trains, and say, we certainly gave her a good time. The mayor read her an address and presented her with a gold-mounted polished cow's-foot combination ink-well, thermometer, and daily text calendar that I'll bet she's showing the folks in her palace right now."

On religion: "I tell you, I'm as religious as the next fellow, and I never'd for one moment dream of criticizing the preachers' doctrines—let them figure out theology and religion, I say, and I'll stick to the office-supply business. But don't it sometimes almost make you question the workings of Providence when you see the mysterious way in which disease smites down the just with the unjust?"

On Global Warming in 1928: "Seems to me that on the whole the world has gotten warmer than it used to be when we were kids. You read in the papers how it hasn't changed materially, but they can say what they want to, don't you remember how doggone cold it used to be in the mornings when we had to get up and chase off to school, and now it seems like we don't have any more old-fashioned winters—maybe that's one reason why the kids today aren't as self-reliant as we were—"

On eating at a restaurant: "'My God,' I says to one of these smart-aleck headwaiters, or maybe he was what they call a captain, anyway he was the fellow that takes the order and then he hands it on to the regular waiter. 'My God,' I said to him, when I looks at the prices on the bill of fare, 'I just come in here to eat,' I says. 'I don't want to buy the hotel!'"

PART TWO: THE STORY OF MACK MCMACK

On the one cafeteria Lowell ate at: "Say, I don't know where you boys were born, and I wouldn't want to hurt anybody's feelings, but my experience is that the cafeterias in Los Angeles are the best in the world, bar none!"

Still on the one cafeteria where Lowell dined: "And after supper, as you left the place, every man was presented with a free cigarette, two toothpicks and a copy of the Gospel of St. Mark; and every lady was presented with a peppermint candy in a glassy-paper wrapper, and a free powder puff, all free."

On birth control: "One faction claims that the superior classes like ourselves, in fact the great British stock, had ought to produce as many kids as possible, to keep in control of this great nation and maintain the ideals for which we and our ancestors have always stood, while these lower masses hadn't ought to spawn their less intellectual masses. But then again, there's them that hold and maintain that now we've cut down immigration, we need a supply of cheap labor, and where get it better than by encouraging these Wops and Hunks and Spigs and so on to raise as many brats as they can?"

On fitness: "That's the one thing to which I attribute my own success and the ability to think quickly and dispose of the day's rush of business without a lot of mental puttering: the fact that I take regular exercise. There's scarcely a day goes by that I don't walk from my office to the Zenith Athletic Club for lunch, and that's not less than a half a mile each way, and every single Sunday from May to November I either have a good round of golf or I'm out driving in the fresh air."

PART THREE: YOU KNOW HOW WOMEN ARE

"Everybody ought to have a rich, full sex-life, and all human activities are directed toward that. Whenever a guy is doing something, it's directed toward making himself attractive sexually, especially if it's something big and important—no matter whether it's painting a picture or putting over a big deal in Florida town-lots or discovering a new eclipse or pitching in a World Series game or preaching a funeral sermon or writing a big advertisement or any of them things. On the other hand, when fellows like us *do* put over something, we want to be appreciated, and we got a right to expect it, and if we don't get appreciated at home, we ought to find new mates, see how I mean?"

"I tell you, Walt, I'm kind of puzzled. Sometimes I almost kind of wonder (though I wound't want to be quoted) whether with all the great things we got in this greatest nation in the world, with more autos and radios and furnaces and suits of clothes and miles of cement pavements and skyscrapers than the rest of the world put together, and with more learning—hundreds of thousands of students studying Latin and bookkeeping and doctoring and domestic science and literature and banking and window-dressing—even with all of this, I wonder if we don't lack something in American life when you consider that you almost never see an American married couple that really like each other and like to be with each other?"

PART FOUR: YOU KNOW HOW RELATIVES ARE

(Editor's Note: There is absolutely nothing in Lowell Schmalt's rant to his wife worth presenting here. I believe that Sinclair Lewis would quite agree.)

PART FIVE: TRAVEL IS SO BROADENING

On whether Lowell went to Yellowstone or not: "Now I myself, I didn't quite get to Yellowstone Park. You know, it's a funny thing how many folks in this man's town think I drove clear from Zenith to Yellowstone Park. I've never claimed anything of the kind. It's true that when I gave my little talk before the West Side Bridge Club about my trip, they billed it—and in a brief way the West Side Tidings column of the *Evening Advocate* spoke of it—as an account of a trip clear to Yellowstone Park."

"And say, I certainly do recommend your making the trip. They can say what they want to. Some people claim that reading books is the greatest cultural influence, and still others maintain that you can get the most in the quickest split-second time by listening to lectures, but what I always say is, 'There's nothing more broadening than travel.'"

"We get to thinking, here in Zenith, that everybody, I mean every *normal* fellow, lives just like we do, but out there in Minnesota I found a lot of the folks never even heard of our mayor here in Zenith—they just talked about Minneapolis and Saint Paul politics! I tell you, travel

Michael Fridgen

like that gives a fellow a whole new set of insights into human character and how big the world is, after all, and as our pastor, Dr. Edwards, often says, the capacity of the Lord for producing new sets of psychological set-ups is practically, you might say, absolutely unlimited."

"Yes, thanks, I'll have a cigar, but I'm not drinking anything. Well, make it very mild. Fine, that's fine. After all, as I often tell my boy, Robby, since prohibition *is* a law of the land, we ought to drink nothing at all or only very little."

PART SIX: THE BASIC AND FUNDAMENTAL IDEALS OF CHRISTIAN AMERICAN CITIZENSHIP

On customer service: "And so in other businesses. The grocery customer will often prefer a second-rate apple in a handsome wrapper to a first-rate one carelessly bundled in plain tissue paper. A motorist will stand for pretty bad gasoline if the gas-station employees wear handsome uniforms, greet the customer respectfully, and wipe off his windshield free. A man will often put up with small rooms, high prices, and even pretty poor food if both the reception clerk and the manager treat him like a friend, give him a warm handshake, and, this most especially, learn his name thoroughly and greet him by it when he returns a second time. That's Service!"

On the advancements in advertising: "At last has come the glorious era when every noble sentiment, every artistic turn of phrase and elegant wording, every instinct of beauty, is no longer forced to run alone and maverick, but can rejoicingly take its proper place in serving commerce and the merchant kings!"

In conclusion, finally: "And I shall be glad if in my small way I have done anything to make clearer to you the New Era of American Civilization; to express modestly to you the motto of Lowell Schmaltz: 'Read widely, think scientifically, speak briefly, and sell the goods!'"

Dodsworth (1929)

I will admit one of my inner-most desires: to take a hard-cover copy of *Dodsworth* and use it to smack every Millennial I meet when I travel. Allow me to explain. I'm about as Generation X as one could possibly be. I'm hyper-skeptical of everything. I believe that the Baby Boomers sucked up all the resources and that the Millennials are a bunch of booming babies. Consequently, Sam Dodsworth (clearly the voice of Sinclair Lewis) and I would have been great traveling companions.

Dodsworth is, basically, a statement about the philosophy of travel—or the lack thereof. Lewis was well traveled for one living in the very early 20th century. There is no doubt that much of *Dodsworth* is drawn from his personal experience.

It's quite clear from his writing that Sinclair Lewis hated anyone who was inauthentic and pretentious. Traveling in Europe in 1925, Sam Dodsworth meets many people that are quite inauthentic and unknowingly pretentious—unfortunately, not much has changed in the last one-hundred years. (Again, did Sinclair Lewis have access to H. G. Wells's time machine?)

I'm fortunate that I have the ability and resources to travel extensively. I won't apologize for that, and I'm grateful every day for the life I live. *Dodsworth* is the only book I've read about travel that accurately reflects my experiences. I hold views that are contrary to many I meet: It's okay to want good service; air-conditioning is not of the devil; travelers should not be afraid to be tourists, because those who want to live like locals are just kidding themselves because they are not locals; and there are a few good things about the United States of America. (The looks I get from Millennial travelers when I say something good about the U.S.A. could kill many cats.)

Like the rest of the Sinclair Lewis library, *Dodsworth* requires a lot of the reader, particularly if that reader is also a traveler. Is there a place for the traveler who merely wants to be a traveler and not a resident? Millennials are advised to stay clear of this book. But for those of us that love to see new things, have fun, and then retreat to our comfortable homes, *Dodsworth* is pure heaven.

CHAPTER 2

To define what Sam Dodsworth was, at fifty, it is easiest to state what he was not. He was none of the things which most Europeans and many Americans expect in a leader of American industry. He was not a Babbitt, not a Rotarian, not an Elk, not a deacon. He rarely shouted, never slapped people on the back, and he had attended only six baseball games since 1900. He knew, and thoroughly, the Babbitts and baseball fans, but only in business.

CHAPTER 2

On Sam Dodsworth selling his business: He was not happy about it, when he let himself think abstractly. But he was extremely well trained, from his first days in Zenith High School, in not letting himself do anything so destructive as abstract thinking.

CHAPTER 3

Sam Dodsworth: "I'd like," Sam reflected, "to sit under a linden tree for six straight months and not hear one word about Efficiency or Doing Big Things or anything more important than the temperature of the beer—if there is anything more important."

CHAPTER 3

Tub Pearson on Dodsworth's Plan to travel in Europe: "Six months! Oh, don't be a damn' fool! Go for two months, and then you'll be able to appreciate getting back to a country where you can get ice and a bath-tub."

CHAPTER 4

Fran Dodsworth: "In Europe, a woman at forty is just getting to the age where important men take a serious interest in her. But here, she's a grandmother."

CHAPTER 5

A racing view of all their companions of the voyage, their fellow-citizens in this brave village amid the desert of waters: strangers to be hated on sight, to be snubbed lest they snub first, yet presently to be known better and better loved and longer remembered than neighbors seen for a lifetime on the cautious land.

CHAPTER 5

On Sam Dodsworth meeting his first European: Sam had the American yearning to become acquainted, to tell all about his achievements, not as boasting but to establish himself as a worthy fellow.

CHAPTER 6

Like most people who have never traveled abroad, Sam had not emotionally believed that these "foreign scenes" veritably existed; that human beings really could live in environments so different from the front yards of Zenith suburbs; that Europe was anything save a fetching myth like the Venusberg. But finding it actually visible, he gave himself up to grasping it as enthusiastically as, these many years, he had given himself to grinding out motor cars.

CHAPTER 7

Fran Dodsworth on England: "I'm sorry. I was naughty. I'm sorry." Then she laughed. "Only my people didn't come from here! My revered ancestors galloped around the Bavarian mountains in short green pants, and yodeled, and undoubtedly they fought your ancestors on all possible occasions!"

CHAPTER 7

Dodsworth on a colleague: "He's cocky, and I don't suppose he's read a book since he used to look at the lingerie ads in the Sears-Roebuck catalogue as a kid, but he's a whirlwind at selling, and he tells mighty good stories, and he would know the best restaurants in London."

CHAPTER 7

He felt, at the theater, even more forlorn. He did not understand more than two-thirds of what the actors said on the stage. He had been brought up to believe that the English language and the American language were one, but what could a citizen of Zenith make of "Ohs rath, eastill in labtry"?

CHAPTER 8

Sam had never, for all of Fran's years of urging that it was a genteel and superior custom, been able to get himself to enjoy breakfast in bed. It seemed messy. Prickly crumbs of toast crept in between the sheets, honey got itself upon his pajamas, and it was impossible to enjoy an honest cup of coffee unless he squared up to it at an honest table.

CHAPTER 9

He wanted to escape from the hotel-and-theater London of the tourist and see the authentic English—Dorset shepherds—cotton operatives on the dole in Salford—collier captains in Bristol harbor—Cornish tin-miners—Cambridge dons—hop-pickers in Kentish pubs—great houses in the Dukeries. But they were too low or too high for Fran's attention, and was it probable, he sighed, that he would see anything that she did not choose?

CHAPTER 9

Lockert (a European): "Americans understand themselves less and are less understood by the world than any nation that's ever existed. You're excellent at all the things in which you're supposed to be lacking—lyric poetry, formal manners, lack of cupidity. And you're so timid and incompetent at the things in which you're supposed to excel—fast motoring, aviation, efficiency in business, pioneering—why, Britain has done more pioneering, in Canada and Africa and Australia and China, in any given ten years, than the States have in twenty."

Main Speak: Quotes from the Work of Sinclair Lewis

CHAPTER 10

Because of the British fetish of unannotated introductions, Sam never did learn the profession of Mr. Alls (if that was his name) and naturally, to an American, the profession of a stranger is a more important matter than even his income, his opinion of Socialism, his opinion of Prohibition, or the make of his motor car.

CHAPTER 10

Herndon: "The trouble with this country is," observed Herndon, "that there're too many people going about saying: 'The trouble with this country is—'"

CHAPTER 11

Sam Dodsworth: "Sorry if it's bad manners not to be ashamed of being an American, but then I'll just have to be bad mannered!"

CHAPTER 11

Sam Dodsworth: "What's the idea of coming to a famous city and then not seeing the places that made it famous? You don't have to send souvenir cards about 'em if you don't want to!"

CHAPTER 12

Paris is one of the largest, and certainly it is the pleasantest, of modern American cities. It is a joyous town, and its chief joy is in its jealousies. Every citizen is in rivalry with all the others in his knowledge of French, of museums, of wine, and of restaurants.

CHAPTER 13

He found that in certain French bathrooms one can have hot water without waiting for a geyser. He found that he needn't have brought two dozen tubes of his favorite (and very smelly) toothpaste from America—one actually could buy toothpaste, corn-plasters, New York Sunday papers, Bromo-Seltzer, Lucky Strikes, safety razor blades, and ice cream almost as easily in Paris as in the United States; and a man he met at Luigi's Bar insisted that if one quested earnestly enough, he could find B.V.D.'s.

CHAPTER 14

Lycurgus (or Jerry) Watts was the professional amateur of Zenith. He was a large-faced man, as wide as a truck-driver, but he had a whiney, caressing voice, and he giggled at his own jokes, which were incessant and very bad. He was reputed to be fifty years old, and he looked anywhere from twenty-five to a hundred.

CHAPTER 14

Sam Dodsworth: "So far as I can see," he brooded, "travel consists in perpetually finding new things that you have to do if you're going to be respectable."

CHAPTER 15

Ross Ireland: "Oh, Paris! Paris is nothing but a post-graduate course in Broadway. Paris is a town for Americans that can't stand work."

CHAPTER 16

Then there were the customs. Not that the inspectors were so impolite as is fabled, but it is irritating to be suspected of smuggling liquor, particularly when, like Sam, you are smuggling liquor.

CHAPTER 16

Ross Ireland: "I've been going around Europe and Asia telling the heathen that the reason we hustle so in New York is because we get so much done. I never discovered till today that we do all this hustling, all this jamming in subways, all this elbowing into elevators, to keep ourselves occupied and keep from getting anything done!"

CHAPTER 16

Ross Ireland: "Honestly, Sam, I don't get these here United States. We let librarians censor all the books, and yet we have musical comedies like this—just as raw as Paris. We go around hollering that we're the only bona fide friends of democracy and self-determination, and yet with Haiti and Nicaragua we're doing everything we accused Germany of doing in Belgium, and—you mark my word—within a year we'll be starting a Big Navy campaign for the purpose of bullying the world as Great Britain never thought of doing. We boast of scientific investigation, and yet we're the only supposedly civilized country where thousands of supposedly sane citizens will listen to an illiterate clod-hopping preacher or politician setting himself up as an authority on biology and attacking evolution."

CHAPTER 19

He'd gone abroad to seek; all the scarlets and yellows and frivolous pinks, all the twisty iron-work and scalloped tiles and striped awnings and Sicilian wine-jars he could swallow, along with (he thanked Heaven) all the mass-produced American electric refrigerators, oil furnaces, vacuum cleaners, garbage incinerators, over-stuffed chairs and built-in garages which, for all of Fran's scoffing and Mr. Atkins' expatriate distress, Sam still approved.

CHAPTER 20

Fran Dodsworth: "But not marry him. He's too much like plum cake—wonderful at a Christmas feast, but he'd bring indigestion. For a permanent diet I'd prefer good, honest, dependable bread—which you are—please don't think that's insulting; it's really a great compliment."

CHAPTER 21

Since the days of Alexander the Great there has been a fashionable belief that travel is agreeable and highly educative. Actually, it is one of the most arduous yet boring of all pastimes and, except in the case of a few experts who go globe-trotting for special purposes, it merely provides the victim with more topics about which to show ignorance.

CHAPTER 21

He who has seen one cathedral ten times has seen something; he who has seen ten cathedrals once has seen but little; and he who has spent half an hour in each of a hundred cathedrals has seen nothing at all. Four hundred pictures all on a wall are four hundred times less interesting than one picture; and no one knows a cafe till he has gone there often enough to know the names of the waiters.

CHAPTER 21

If travel were so inspiring and informing a business as the new mode of round-the-world-tour advertisements eloquently sets forth, then the wisest men in the world would be deck hands on tramp steamers, Pullman porters, and Mormon missionaries.

CHAPTER 21

Actually, most of those afflicted with the habit of traveling merely lie about its pleasures and profits. They do not travel to see anything, but to get away from themselves, which they never do, and away from rowing with their relatives—only to find new relatives with whom to row.

CHAPTER 22

Now he admitted that in all of Europe, however interesting other nationals, however merry the Italians and keen the French, he found only the British and the Germans his own sort of people. With them alone could he understand what they thought, how they lived, and what they wanted of life.

CHAPTER 23

And before she had ever left America she had been able to point her Europeanism by keeping her fork in her left hand. But now she added to her accomplishments the ability to make a European 7 by crossing it, and ardently she crossed every 7, particularly in letters to friends in Zenith, who were thus prevented from knowing what figure she was using.

CHAPTER 23

Sam Dodsworth: "Well, I'll bet the French peasant that sticks the centimes away in the sock, and the German farmer, love the dollar ten times as much as the average American. We love to make money, but we love to spend it. We're all like sailors on a spree."

CHAPTER 25

Fran Dodsworth: "When the world hears the word 'grandmother,' it pictures an old woman, a withered old woman, who's absolutely hors de combat. I'm not that and I'm not going to be, for another twenty years. And YET, most people are so conventional-minded that even if they know me, see me, dance with me, once they hear I'm a grandmother that label influences them more than their own senses, and they put me on the side-lines immediately."

CHAPTER 26
Matey Pearson: "Oh, I am so tired, Sam, of hearing and reading about these modern folks—you get 'em in every novel—these sensitive plants that go around being rude and then stand back complacently and explain that it's because they're so SHY!"

CHAPTER 27
A man alone at a cafe table in the more intellectual portions of Paris, and not apparently expecting some one, is always a man suspect. At home he may be a prince, a successful pickpocket, or an explorer, but in this city of necessitous and over-friendly strollers, this city where any one above the rank of assassin or professional martyr can so easily find companions, the supposition is that he is alone because he ought to be alone.

CHAPTER 30
But between blurred drowsinesses, he saw with clarity that he was utterly a man alone, that his work, his children, his friends, his habitual routine of life, and at last his wife, all the props and crutches with which he had been enabled to hobble through life as a Good Fellow, were gone, and that he had nothing upon which to depend except such solaces as he might find in his own brain. No one really needed him, and he was a man who had never been able to depend on any one to whom he could not give.

CHAPTER 30
He had known unhappiness often enough, but never complete suffering like this—a suffering so vague and directionless and unreasonable that he raged at himself for his moody weakness—a suffering so confusing that he would have preferred any definite pain of the body.

Michael Fridgen

CHAPTER 31

Sam's spirit was refreshed here, his hot body was refreshed, and when Mrs. Cortright showed herself so superior to Expatriate Americanism that she dared to be American and to offer iced tea, he rejoiced in her more than in the mosaics of St. Mark's, which he had taught himself to admire with a quite surprising amount of sincerity.

CHAPTER 32

Edith Cortright: "All the complications are inside myself. It's just that certain conditions of life have rather taken my confidence in myself away from me, and I'm so afraid of doing the wrong thing that it's easier to do nothing."

CHAPTER 33

The driver of their taxi, being Neapolitan, was in a rage so long as any vehicle was on the road ahead of him, and as that was always, their journey was a series of escapes from death.

CHAPTER 34

Edith Cortright: "The trouble with the rich American is that he feels uncouth and untraditional, and so he meekly trots to Europe to buy sun-dials and Fifteenth Century mantelpieces and refectory tables—to try to buy aristocracy by buying the aristocrats' worn-out coats. I like my Europe in Europe; at home I'd like to watch people make something new. For example, your motor cars."

CHAPTER 36

Edith Cortright: "What a job it is to give up the superiority of being miserable and self-sacrificing!"

Ann Vickers (1933)

The Sinclair Lewis Interpretive Center was a small flat building just off Interstate 94 in Sauk Centre, Minnesota. It doesn't exist any longer as the city reclaimed the property with the hope that its prominent position along the highway would attract a fast-food restaurant. The property remains unsold to this day. But the sale is not a bad thing–the museum had fallen into disrepair. There is, however, renewed interest in bringing the artifacts from the interpretive center to a new facility right on Main Street and near the Sinclair Lewis Boyhood Home. In fact, an old creamery has been purchased and renovations will begin shortly. (In *Main Street* language, shortly means anytime between now and the next Millennium.)

I have good reason to mention the interpretive center in the introduction to *Ann Vickers*. The original Sinclair Lewis Interpretive Center contained large displays of what the museum called "The Big Five". I have no idea who designed the display and I've never encountered the phrase "The Big Five" associated with Sinclair Lewis in any other venue. It seems to have been a construct just for the interpretive center. "The Big Five", according to the museum, were: *Main Street, Babbitt, Elmer Gantry, Arrowsmith*, and *Dodsworth*.

"The Big Five" bothered me because I thought *Ann Vickers* deserved to be listed with them. *Ann Vickers* was written around the same time as the other five and the scope of the novel is just as epic. However, it didn't sell nearly as many copies. The subject was taboo for the readers of 1933: Ann Vickers is a strong, intelligent woman who dares to control her own destiny. *Ann Vickers* was just too far ahead of its time–had this novel been written twenty years later, Sinclair Lewis would have won another Pulitzer Prize.

Ann Vickers is a feminist. But unlike activists of the modern age, she's willing to expend enormous amounts of energy to educate herself on the complexity of the problems facing society. She's hard-working enough to get her hands dirty, and she's smart enough to befriend the right people in power. She's simply amazing and I wish I could be her friend. (Surely, Ann Vickers needs a gay best friend like no other woman in literature!)

The subject of abortion is masterfully dissected by Sinclair Lewis in this work. In current times, the discussion of abortion has been corrupted by people on both sides of the political spectrum. In Lewis's work, abortion has more than two sides. It's complicated. Women in the novel make decisions and live with them. Sometimes there is regret and other times there is relief. Often, there is a mixture of both. There is no doubt that Lewis, in 1933, believed that abortion was too complicated and personal to belong to politicians.

Another major theme of *Ann Vickers* is prison reform. Ann begins adult life as a social worker and devotes her career to the criminal justice system of the 1920's. It's heart wrenching to read. There are no easy answers here. Actually, I believe that Ann would say there *are* easy answers, but we don't want to try them because we're afraid they may work.

In the midst of all this reform, Ann Vickers is still a person who yearns and loves her way through life. She doesn't always make the best choices when it comes to men, but in her defense, she's so far ahead of her time that like-minded mates are few and far between.

Sometimes, I like to think that Ann is actually Carol Kennicott's daughter from *Main Street*. I don't know that the timing and geography really work out, but Carol would have been so proud of Ann. (Good Lord! Dr. Will Kennicott would never have survived having Ann Vickers for a daughter.) Regardless, Ann deserves to take her place beside Carol, George, Elmer, Martin, and Sam as part of "The Big Six".

CHAPTER 1
But Ann had the extraordinary luck (along with some 120,000,000 other Americans) to live in the magnificent though appalling moment when the United States began awkwardly to see itself not as an illegitimate child of Europe but as the master of its own proud house.

CHAPTER 2
It was perhaps the first time in the life of Ann Vickers that a grown-up had talked to her as an equal; it was perhaps the first time in her life that she had been invited to consider any social problem more complicated than the question as to whether girls really ought to throw dead cats over fences. It was perhaps the beginning of her intellectual life.

CHAPTER 4
Mildred Evans: "Jiminy, Ann Vickers is funny," observed Mildred Evans. "She's crazy! She says she don't want to get married. She wants to be a doctor or a lawyer or somethin', I dunno. She's crazy!"

CHAPTER 6
Dr. Hargis: "And in the early days of America, when bathing was just coming in, there were sages who explained that Rome fell solely because the Roman dandies took to daily hot bathing. But none of these retrospective prophets ever consider the fact that actually Rome never did fall! Rome did not fall! Rome *changed!*"

CHAPTER 8
Ann Vickers: "I'm not shocked at all! Good heavens, this is the modern age! It's not 1890! I've studied biology. But one doesn't do these things lightly. I'd have a lover, if I wanted him enough, that particular him!"

CHAPTER 12

On the fictional small city of Tafford: It was, like Hartford, Conn., or any American city named Springfield, so conservative that it resembled an English cathedral town, minus the cathedral.

CHAPTER 13

Perhaps, she sighed (looking at one of the cockroaches, which bred faster than they could slap them to death)—perhaps she was one of the Marthas who could never be so showily wasteful as to anoint the world with the spikenard of sexual exaltation, who would always be serving the dinner for Lazarus and Jesus, who would be for and of the mass, and never an "individual."

CHAPTER 14

The Corlears Hook Settlement House entered the war along with President Wilson. Like the great Socialist thinker, Mr. Upton Sinclair, all the settlement workers except Ann proclaimed that while they were pacifists, opposed to all other wars, *this* crusade was to overthrow the Prussian military clique, after which there would forever be universal peace.

CHAPTER 14

He kissed her at the door, and she stood in the corridor, she was dizzy and astonished with the fire of that kiss, in which all her individuality had been burnt away, so that for a second she had not been a separate person, but one flesh with him, fused in an electric flare.

CHAPTER 15

She had thought, she had even said, to Eula Towers and to Pat Bramble, that there must be something sickeningly vulgar about a man's shaving. If *she* ever married, all those sordidnesses would be shut away, in bathrooms!

CHAPTER 16

On Ann's neighborhood revue: "The credit went to the Broadway manager, who had spent one hour on the scheme, to Ann Vickers, who had spend perhaps ten hours, to the head-resident, who had spent none at all, and not to the native authors, nor to the cast, who had worked from 8 p.m. till three in the morning every night for a month.

CHAPTER 17

Just as it is a felony to help a condemned murderer cheat the state of its beloved blood-letting by passing poison to him, so that he may die decently and alone, with no sadistic parade of priests and guards and reporters, so is it a crime to assist a woman condemned to the tittering gossip that can be worse than death by helping her avoid having what is quaintly known as an "illegitimate baby"—as though one should speak of an "illegitimate mountain" or an "illegitimate hurricane." A physician who keeps a rich woman abed and nervous is a great and good man; a physician who saves a girl from disgrace is an intruder who, having stolen from society the pleasure of viciousness, is rightly sent to prison.

CHAPTER 18

Dr. Malvina Wormser: "Women are the first, the natural docs. It's they that bind up the baby's finger and plan his diet; it's they that have patience and endurance. It's they that take pain seriously, as something that must be gotten rid of—most men doctors (except Jewish ones, who have brains!) say that 'pain is perfectly normal, so why worry about it'—that is, when the pain is in somebody else's belly—a man doctor is just as scared as any of his patients when it's in his own belly—worst patient in the world, a man doc!"

CHAPTER 19

Eleanor Crevecoeur: "Women, cats, and elephants are the only animals with sense."

CHAPTER 19

Dr. Herringdean: "Isn't it curious," she complained, "that in 1918, in the age of Freud and ragtime and little war-widows, the view about women, even among women themselves, is still that they are angels, lacking all organs except hearts and lungs and rudimentary brains!"

CHAPTER 21

On Ann being propositioned by a man: He managed to insinuate "Let's sleep together" even when he said, "I saw a porpoise this morning." Ann did not, theoretically, mind being seduced again. Nice time for it, vacation, with no lecture engagements. But she did object to being not an individual woman, but merely a coupon.

CHAPTER 22

Dr. Jelke: "At its best, any prison is so unnatural a form of segregation from normal life that–like too-loving parents and too-zealous religion and all other well-meant violations of individuality–it helps to prevent the victims from resuming, when they are let out, any natural role in human society."

CHAPTER 22

Dr. Jelke: "Prison makes the man who hates his bosses come out hating everyone. Prison makes a man who is sexually abnormal, sexually a maniac. Prison makes the man who enjoyed beating fellow-drunks in a barroom come out wanting to kill a policeman."

CHAPTER 25

Josiah Flint: "There are no tramps–there are only men tramping," said Josiah Flint. And there are no doctors–only men studying medicine; there are no authors–only men writing; there are no criminals and no prisoners, but only men who have done something that at the moment was regarded as breaking the law, and who at the hit-or-miss-guess-verdict of a judge (who was no judge at all, but only a man judging, in accordance as his digestion and his wife's nagging affected him) were carted off to a prison.

CHAPTER 26

Kittie Cognac: "I dunno. I guess in some ways I haven't been a very good woman. You see, my Dad hated me. Well, all right, all right! I'll show him! He's been dead these twenty years, but I'll show him! To get even with him, I'm going to take it out on every living man I can get my hooks on!"

CHAPTER 27

On the execution of Lil Hezekiah: By the grace of God Amen in our Christian nation wherein we rage not as the Heathen but under the gentle teachings of Jesus do combine in one grand union for the purpose of gently murdering skinny old colored mammies let us now sing the Land of the Free and the Home of the Brave—

CHAPTER 27

Dr. Sorella on the execution of Lil Hezekiah: "In fact, if there is to be any capital punishment at all, I'd give the poor devils a chance to commit suicide, decently and unobserved; hand 'em some poison they could take when they wanted to. But as it is, I don't dare even give them morphia. In the old days the warden would get a condemned prisoner nice and drunk, so he swung off happily. But the preachers and Good People of this state decided that their God wouldn't get enough relish out of His vengeance if the sinners weren't sober, and aware what He was doing to them."

CHAPTER 27

The two women heaved the body into the coffin, slammed on the cover, and cheerfully marched out, leaving Lil Hezekiah to her relatives and to God. But later the relatives failed to return, and she was buried in the jail yard. What God did is not known.

CHAPTER 28

Fortunately, Ann was a professionally trained uplifter. She had learned in settlement two things: that she must not expect "gratitude," and that people who did expect gratitude were the eternal amateurs, the eternal egoists.

CHAPTER 30

Editor Charley Erman: "A newspaper's worst trouble is with people that don't want something for themselves but for the world."

CHAPTER 33

Dr. Wormser: "Good heaven, Ann, it's world-old. It's the story of Aristides the Just. Three fourths of the mass hate superior people.

Verily I saw unto you, there shall be more rejoicing over one good man pulled down to the mob than over nine and ninety that are elevated for an example to mankind."

CHAPTER 36

The cards were stacked again you, Ann. No doubt they will be against your great-great-granddaughter. But since birth and life have thrust you into the game, at least be warned that the cards have been stacked.

CHAPTER 38

The word "party" indicated, in that ultimate climax of civilization, 1930 in New York, many things. To the artistic, it meant gin and necking. To the raucously inartistic, it meant gin and necking. To persons so rich and respectable that they had not yet begun to whimper about the "Depression" that was just begun, it meant contract bridge and gin. But to the forward-looking group, it meant just Talk.

CHAPTER 41

The Great Depression did not depress Ann. It strangely exhilarated her. She saw poverty again accepted as natural and non-mortal.

CHAPTER 47

Ann was astonished to discover how much money she could make when, for the first time in her life, she gave attention to this dull art. She concluded that the chief quality of millionaires was not their orderly planning, their gift of selecting assistants, not their imaginative forecasting of the world's future needs in such fascinating matters as gasoline and pocket-flasks and oatmeal in red packages, but just their being stupid enough to want to sacrifice living to money-making.

Work of Art (1934)

Sinclair Lewis was obsessed with the hotel industry. Hotels and the future of lodging are themes that appear in several of his works. Having been born in 1885, Lewis was in a position to see the world change like no previous generation had. This was all due, mainly, to the advent of the automobile.

As I stated earlier, there is no doubt that smart phones changed the world. But they changed *how* we do things. Automobiles changed *what* we do–they changed our very nature. Massive industries, non-virtual, sprung up to support a population that was, for the first time, individually mobile. Those who went driving required lodging. However, they needed something that was between the grand city hotels and the small-town boarding house.

Work of Art is a fascinating look at the birth of the hotel industry. The story is seen through the eyes of Myron Weagle as he obsessively strives to do his best at whatever he's doing. Using a brilliant device, Sinclair Lewis contrasts Myron's life with that of his brother Ora, a struggling writer. My husband, the other Lewis that I mentioned earlier, is a psychiatrist and firmly believes that *Work of Art* is Sinclair Lewis's best work. The portrayals of Myron and Ora are so convincing that even their psychological issues are fully on display.

In *Work of Art*, Sinclair Lewis mostly refrains from using satire against the hotel industry itself. Instead, he employs his signature satirical style against the functions of society that can make guests and hoteliers annoying. Little has changed since this book was written. I still see Myron's guests anytime I visit the complementary continental breakfast at a mid-priced chain hotel along the interstate.

While the story moves around the United States a bit, much of it takes place in large New York City hotels. This is the same time and place as *Ann Vickers*, and Dr. Wormser makes a cameo appearance. The problems that Myron encounters with guests are scandalous, humorous, and sometimes sad. Prohibition is a minor theme in the book. Myron, as did all hoteliers of the time, reluctantly works around the complexities of this strange time in American History.

Above all, *Work of Art* is a story about obsession. It's better told and much easier to read than *Moby Dick*, but the benefits and consequences of obsession are just as apparent for Myron as they are for Ahab.

CHAPTER 1
In the hall he met Flossy Gitts, the second maid. Now Ora was fifteen and Flossy was twenty, but she was generous and without prejudice: she had ringlets and what was then known as a bust; she dallied happily with any male from the age of ten to one hundred, though she preferred a ripe traveling-man of thirty-five, who wore a Masonic ring and was willing to hire a liberty stable rig to give a girl a good time.

CHAPTER 2
It was called 'Elm Hill', naturally it was covered mostly with spruce and pine.

CHAPTER 3
It is one of life's ironies that the suggestion of a passer-by–a man met on a train, the unknown author of an editorial, an actor repeating a pure and pompous sentiment in a melodrama–may be weightier than years of boring advice by parents.

CHAPTER 6
In all the Black Thread High School there was no boy more popular than Myron Weagle. Yet he had no friends. For in boyhood, friendships are strictly based on leisure hours. Friends are the companions of your evening games of pom-pom-pullaway and prisoner's base, of Saturday

afternoon hikes through the woods, of lolling at the swimming hole. They need have, these friends of boyhood, no two thoughts in common with you, nor any similarity of taste; met after a lapse of twenty years, they may be stranger than any chance acquaintance of yesterday in the Pullman car. They are comrades at arms, not intimates. And thus, having no leisure in boyhood, Myron could have no friends.

CHAPTER 9
Herbert Lambkin: "Oh. Yes. Well–have a chair! Have two chairs!" This was advanced collegiate humour, in 1901, and possibly in 1931.

CHAPTER 9
It had always been reputed throughout Connecticut that all 'Yale men' were young gods, with athletic prowess and awe-inspiring wealth. Myron now perceived that they were extraordinarily like human beings.

CHAPTER 10
He signed the letter 'Myron S. Weagle'. The 'S' in his name stood for nothing whatever. He had put it in three years before because, obviously, a successful man can't go about naked, with no middle initial.

CHAPTER 13
The chary world gives credit to Homer and Hippocrates and Gutenberg and the Wright Brothers and Edison and Ivy Lee, inventor of government by propaganda, but no one remembers the originators of really important details of life–the discoverers of fire and coffee and the wheel, the inventors of the pocket handkerchief and cigarettes, the innovators who first discovered that man can sleep from midnight till eight instead of from six to two, or the creators, like Myron, of the first enticing and flattering sales-letters.

CHAPTER 19
On Myron and Fffie's engagement: He never did propose. It is, indeed, doubtful whether anybody in history, outside of novels, ever has really 'proposed'. They simply came to know that they liked each other and excited each other, and that, presumably, they were going to be married.

CHAPTER 20

Carlos Jaynes suggested that, though for their Buffalo, Worcester, Akron, Hartford and Scranton houses, English menus were all right, it would give what he called 'cachet' to the Westward to have menus, at least in the Georgian Dining Room, in French. On the sample which Jaynes submitted, Myron found the item, 'Le ham and eggs'. Now that was perfectly sound, for had Jaynes not taken it from the menu of the Savoy Grill, in London?"

CHAPTER 20

Then the convention. The arrival of kings, field-marshals, and archbishops, each expecting suitable reverence: the president of the state organization, the secretary, the chairman of the committee on meetings, the chairman of the accommodations committee, the chairman of the banquet committee. Delegates flooding in, demanding rooms they have forgotten to reserve. Lobbies jammed with men slowly circling and exchanging remarks, flasks, and chewing gum, and agreeing that a three-hundred-room hotel which cannot take care of two hundred extra guests at the last moment is not enterprising, and they certainly will never come *here* again! Secretaries of committees, sitting at small desks in large rooms off the lobby, with so many delegates surging about them that they become deaf and blind, and are sometimes found weeks afterward, hiding under the pile of unanswered messages.

CHAPTER 22

Myron often looked at you but did not seem to see you. Ora usually saw you but did not seem to look at you.

CHAPTER 27

On Myron's sympathy toward Ora: He had always felt guilty at doing so little for Ora, who just now happened to be rather hard up, having lost his job as editor and advertising manager of the Hidden Sex Truths Book Publishing Company for having offered to teach hidden sex truths to the stenographers.

It Can't Happen Here (1935)

As reported by *Time Magazine*, within one week of the 2016 US Presidential election, all copies of Sinclair Lewis's *It Can't Happen Here* were sold-out on both Amazon.com and Books-a-Million. For many people, *It Can't Happen Here* is the most terrifying American novel ever written. For some people, it's a silly book. (To spell it out: Those who were saddened by the 2016 result will find the novel terrifying; those who were happy with the 2016 election will find the novel silly.) I won't divulge which side of the argument I'm on (although savvy readers can most accurately guess), regardless, the book is captivating.

Doremus Jessup is the editor of a newspaper in a mid-size Vermont city. It's 1936 and an election is right around the corner. A prominent senator from an unknown state, Buzz Windrip, throws his hat in the ring. Windrip is a populist. He's crass, uneducated, and downright rude. Windrip has written a bestseller called *Zero Hour*; several sections from *Zero Hour* are presented in *It Can't Happen Here*.

Candidate Windrip appeals to the lowest common denominator. His "League of Forgotten Men" is formed among the many citizens who are afraid of immigrants, Jews, women, Blacks, people who can read...and pretty much everyone else. However, it's the middle of the Great American Depression, and voters are enthralled with Windrip's main campaign promise: to give every family $5,000 cash. According to the Bureau of Labor Statistics, $5,000 of money in 1936 has the purchasing power of $91,307 today.

Windrip has a plan to raise the enormous sum required to fulfill this promise–he will raise tariffs against foreign states. The majority of the citizenry agree with him and he is elected.

President Windrip subsequently bribes half of Congress and imprisons the rest. He reorganizes the Supreme Court and within weeks of his inauguration, Windrip is granted emergency powers to become the absolute leader of the United States. His League of Forgotten Men are reorganized under the guise of the terrible M.M. (a.k.a., the Minute Men). Forced labor camps are created as fast as newspapers and schools are dismantled.

Among all this, Doremus Jessup faces the task of living. While the story of Windrip is terrifying, it's actually the "B" story of the novel. The day-to-day struggle of the Jessup family to survive, let alone find happiness, is the main tale of *It Can't Happen Here*. One of the problems with Doremus Jessup is that he's an educated journalist. Another problem is that he has a family. The biggest problem is that he cares.

There is a lot going on in this book. For me, the most amazing aspect of *It Can't Happen Here* is that it was written in 1935. Lewis wrote this novel before the world knew of the full extent of the Nazi war crimes in Germany. The fact that Sinclair Lewis wrote this book without the blueprint of Nazi fascism is nothing short of brilliant.

There is one quote that will not be listed among my selections—and that's because it doesn't exist. Sinclair Lewis is often attributed as having said, "When fascism comes to America it will be wrapped in a flag and carrying a cross." I've even seen it on bumper stickers. And, more than that, I've seen this quote attributed to coming directly from *It Can't Happen Here*. While Lewis would probably have agreed with the quote's sentiment, there is no evidence that he ever said these exact words. This quote is definitely not found within *It Can't Happen Here*.

A reader *can* internalize and discuss any of the novels of Sinclair Lewis. But *It Can't Happen Here* is one novel that the reader *must* internalize and discuss. This is not a book to read alone in the wilderness–this book requires a communal approach in order for the reader to remain sane.

CHAPTER 1

All of America was serious now, after the seven years of depression since 1929. It was just long enough after the Great War of 1914-18 for the young people who had been born in 1917 to be ready to go to college...or to another war, almost any old war that might be handy.

CHAPTER 1

The D.A.R. (reflected the cynic, Doremus Jessup, that evening) is a somewhat confusing organization–as confusing as Theosophy, Relativity, or the Hindu Vanishing Boy Trick, all three of which it resembles. It is composed of females who spend one half their waking hours boasting of being descended from the seditious American colonists of 1776, and the other and more ardent half in attacking all contemporaries who believe in precisely the principles for which those ancestors struggled.

CHAPTER 2

R. C. Crowley: "Why are you so afraid of the word 'Fascism,' Doremus? Just a word–just a word! And might not be so bad, with all the lazy bums we got panhandling relief nowadays, and living on my income tax and yours–not so worse to have a real Strong Man, like Hitler or Mussolini–like Napoleon or Bismarck in the good old days–and have 'em really run the country and make it efficient and prosperous again."

CHAPTER 4

It was Father Charles Coughlin, of Detroit, who had first thought out the device of freeing himself from any censorship of his political sermons on the Mount by "buying his own time on the air"–it being only in the twentieth century that mankind has been able to buy Time as it buys soap and gasoline. This invention was almost equal, in its effect on all American life and thought, to Henry Ford's early conception of selling cars cheap to millions of people, instead of selling a few as luxuries.

CHAPTER 8

Presidential Candidate Buzz Windrip on religion: "Believing that only under God Almighty, to Whom we render all homage, do we Americans hold our vast Power, we shall guarantee to all persons absolute freedom of religious worship, provided, however, that no atheist, agnostic, believer in Black Magic, nor any Jew who shall refuse to swear allegiance to the New Testament, nor any person of any faith who refuses to take the Pledge to the Flag, shall be permitted to hold any public office or to practice as a teacher, professor, lawyer, judge, or as a physician, except in the category of Obstetrics."

CHAPTER 10

On Lee Sarason, Candidate Windrip's publicist: For Sarason it must be said that in this bedlam of "public relations" he never once used *contact* as a transitive verb.

CHAPTER 11

Sissy Jessup: "Oh, my dears, this beastly election! Beastly! Seems as if it's breaking up every town, every home...My poor Dad! Doremus is just about all in!"

CHAPTER 12

Candidate Buzz Windrip: "I shall not be content till this country can produce every single thing we need, even coffee, cocoa, and rubber, and so keep all our dollars at home. If we can do this and at the same time work up tourist traffic so that foreigners will come from every part of the world to see such remarkable wonders as the Grand Canyon, Glacier and Yellowstone etc. parks, the fine hotels of Chicago, & etc., thus leaving their money here, we shall have such a balance of trade as will go far to carry out my often-criticized yet completely sound idea of from $ 3000 to $ 5000 per year for every single family— that is, I mean every real American family."

Main Speak: Quotes from the Work of Sinclair Lewis

CHAPTER 13

In this acid mood Doremus doubted the efficacy of all revolutions; dared even a little to doubt our two American revolutions–against England in 1776, and the Civil War. For a New England editor to contemplate even the smallest criticism of these wars was what it would have been for a Southern Baptist fundamentalist preacher to question Immortality, the Inspiration of the Bible, and the ethical value of shouting Hallelujah.

CHAPTER 13

He even wondered if, necessarily, it had been such a desirable thing for the Thirteen Colonies to have cut themselves off from Great Britain. Had the United States remained in the British Empire, possibly there would have evolved a confederation that could have enforced World Peace, instead of talking about it. Boys and girls from Western ranches and Southern plantations and Northern maple groves might have added Oxford and York Minster and Devonshire villages to their own domain. Englishmen, and even virtuous Englishwomen, might have learned that persons who lack the accent of a Kentish rectory or of a Yorkshire textile village may yet in many ways be literate; and that astonishing numbers of persons in the world cannot be persuaded that their chief aim in life ought to be to increase British exports on behalf of the stock-holdings of the Better Classes. It is commonly asserted, Doremus remembered, that without complete political independence the United States could not have developed its own peculiar virtues. Yet it was not apparent to him that America was any more individual than Canada or Australia; that Pittsburgh and Kansas City were to be preferred before Montreal and Melbourne, Sydney and Vancouver.

CHAPTER 13

Doremus Jessup: "Is it just possible," he sighed, "that the most vigorous and boldest idealists have been the worst enemies of human progress instead of its greatest creators? Possible that plain men with the humble trait of minding their own business will rank higher in the heavenly hierarchy than all the plumed souls who have shoved their way in among the masses and insisted on saving them?"

CHAPTER 16

On Doremus Jessup's early thoughts of the Windrip presidency: The one thing that most perplexed him was that there could be a dictator seemingly so different from the fervent Hitlers and gesticulating Fascists and the Cæsars with laurels round bald domes; a dictator with something of the earthy American sense of humor of a Mark Twain, a George Ade, a Will Rogers, an Artemus Ward. Windrip could be ever so funny about solemn jaw-drooping opponents, and about the best method of training what he called "a Siamese flea hound." Did that, puzzled Doremus, make him less or more dangerous?

CHAPTER 16

Despite strikes and riots all over the country, bloodily put down by the Minute Men, Windrip's power in Washington was maintained. The most liberal four members of the Supreme Court resigned and were replaced by surprisingly unknown lawyers who called President Windrip by his first name. A number of Congressmen were still being "protected" in the District of Columbia jail; others had seen the blinding light forever shed by the goddess Reason and happily returned to the Capitol. The Minute Men were increasingly loyal—they were still unpaid volunteers, but provided with "expense accounts" considerably larger than the pay of the regular troops. Never in American history had the adherents of a President been so well satisfied; they were not only appointed to whatever political jobs there were but to ever so many that really were not; and with such annoyances as Congressional Investigations hushed, the official awarders of contracts were on the merriest of terms with all contractors...One veteran lobbyist for steel corporations complained that there was no more sport in his hunting—you were not only allowed but expected to shoot all government purchasing-agents sitting.

CHAPTER 17

And they had the Jews and the Negroes to look down on, more and more. The M.M.'s saw to that. Every man is a king so long as he has someone to look down on.

Main Speak: Quotes from the Work of Sinclair Lewis

CHAPTER 17

And, increasingly, the bourgeois counter revolutionists began to escape to Canada; just as once, by the "underground railroad" the Negro slaves had escaped into that free Northern air.

CHAPTER 19

Doremus Jessup: "The tyranny of this dictatorship isn't primarily the fault of Big Business, nor of the demagogues who do their dirty work. It's the fault of Doremus Jessup! Of all the conscientious, respectable, lazy-minded Doremus Jessups who have let the demagogues wriggle in, without fierce enough protest. A few months ago I thought the slaughter of the Civil War, and the agitation of the violent Abolitionists who helped bring it on, were evil. But possibly they had to be violent, because easy-going citizens like me couldn't be stirred up otherwise. If our grandfathers had had the alertness and courage to see the evils of slavery and of a government conducted by gentlemen for gentlemen only, there wouldn't have been any need of agitators and war and blood."

CHAPTER 20

On Doremus Jessup writing with a government overseer: And he continued to be just as sick each time he wrote: "The crowd of fifty thousand people who greeted President Windrip in the university stadium at Iowa City was an impressive sign of the constantly growing interest of all Americans in political affairs," and Staubmeyer changed it to: "The vast and enthusiastic crowd of seventy thousand loyal admirers who wildly applauded and listened to the stirring address of the Chief in the handsome university stadium in beautiful Iowa City, Iowa, is an impressive yet quite typical sign of the growing devotion of all true Americans to political study under the inspiration of the Corpo government."

CHAPTER 20

Under a tyranny, most friends are a liability. One quarter of them turn "reasonable" and become your enemies, one quarter are afraid to stop and speak and one quarter are killed and you die with them. But the blessed final quarter keep you alive.

CHAPTER 20

On a day in late October, suddenly striking in every city and village and back-hill hide-out, the Corpos ended all crime in America forever, so titanic a feat that it was mentioned in the London Times. Seventy thousand selected Minute Men, working in combination with town and state police officers, all under the chiefs of the government secret service, arrested every known or faintly suspected criminal in the country. They were tried under court-martial procedure; one in ten was shot immediately, four in ten were given prison sentences, three in ten released as innocent...and two in ten taken into the M.M.' s as inspectors. There were protests that at least six in ten had been innocent, but this was adequately answered by Windrip's courageous statement: "The way to stop crime is to stop it!"

CHAPTER 21

Sissy Jessup on procreating during tyranny: "Why, the more you really do love children, the more you'll want 'em not to be born, now!"

CHAPTER 22

For the first time in America, except during the Civil War and the World War, people were afraid to say whatever came to their tongues. On the streets, on trains, at theaters, men looked about to see who might be listening before they dared so much as say there was a drought in the West, for someone might suppose they were blaming the drought on the Chief!

CHAPTER 22

Doremus could not have stayed away from the book-burning. It was like seeing for the last time the face of a dead friend. Kindling, excelsior, and spruce logs had been heaped on the thin snow on the Green. (Tomorrow there would be a fine patch burned in the hundred-year-old sward.) Round the pyre danced M.M.'s, schoolboys, students from the rather ratty business college on Elm Street, and unknown farm lads, seizing books from the pile guarded by the broadly cheerful Shad and skimming them into the flames. Doremus saw his Martin Chuzzlewit fly into air and land on the burning lid of an ancient commode. It lay there open to a Phiz drawing of Sairey Gamp, which withered instantly. As a small boy he had always laughed over that drawing.

CHAPTER 24

Doremus Jessup: "I can never forgive evil and lying and cruel means, and still less can I forgive fanatics that use that for an excuse! If I may imitate Romain Rolland, a country that tolerates evil means—evil manners, standards of ethics—for a generation, will be so poisoned that it never will have any good end."

CHAPTER 24

Philip Jessup defending tyranny: "I want to make myself clear. Before Windrip, we'd been lying down in America, while Europe was throwing off all her bonds—both monarchy and this antiquated parliamentary-democratic-liberal system that really means rule by professional politicians and by egotistic 'intellectuals.' We've got to catch up to Europe again—got to expand—it's the rule of life. A nation, like a man, has to go ahead or go backward. Always!"

CHAPTER 25

Day on day he waited. So much of a revolution for so many people is nothing but waiting. That is one reason why tourists rarely see anything but contentment in a crushed population. Waiting, and its brother death, seem so contented.

CHAPTER 26

Doc Itchitt on being a newspaper man during the Windrip Presidency: "And it's a swell régime. Fellow can get ahead in newspaper work now, and not be held back by a bunch of snobs that think they're so doggone educated just because they went to college!"

CHAPTER 26

President Windrip, who was apparently becoming considerably more jumpy than in his old, brazen days, saw two of his personal bodyguard snickering together in the anteroom of his office and, shrieking, snatching an automatic pistol from his desk, started shooting at them. He was a bad marksman. The suspects had to be finished off by the pistols of their fellow guards.

CHAPTER 27

Sissy Jessup on the possibility of being raped by Shad: "Do you honestly suppose that since the New Civilization began, say in 1914, anyone believes that kind of thing is more serious than busting an ankle? 'A fate worse than death'! What nasty old side-whiskered deacon ever invented that phrase? And how he must have rolled it on his chapped old lips! I can think of plenty worse fates—say, years of running an elevator. No—wait! I'm not really flippant. I haven't any desire, beyond maybe a slight curiosity, to be raped—at least, not by Shad; he's a little too strong on the Bodily Odor when he gets excited. (Oh God, darling, what a nasty swine that man is! I hate him fifty times as much as you do. Ugh!) But I'd be willing to have even that happen if I could save one decent person from his bloody blackjack. I'm not the playgirl of Pleasant Hill any more; I'm a frightened woman from Mount Terror!"

CHAPTER 29

Doremus, reading the authors he had concealed in the horsehair sofa—the gallant Communist, Karl Billinger, the gallant anti-Communist, Tchernavin, and the gallant neutral, Lorant—began to see something like a biology of dictatorships, all dictatorships. The universal apprehension, the timorous denials of faith, the same methods of arrest—sudden pounding on the door late at night, the squad of police pushing in, the blows, the search, the obscene oaths at the frightened women, the third degree by young snipe of officials, the accompanying blows and then the formal beatings, when the prisoner is forced to count the strokes until he faints, the leprous beds and the sour stew, guards jokingly shooting round and round a prisoner who believes he is being executed, the waiting in solitude to know what will happen, till men go mad and hang themselves—Thus had things gone in Germany, exactly thus in Soviet Russia, in Italy and Hungary and Poland, Spain and Cuba and Japan and China. Not very different had it been under the blessings of liberty and fraternity in the French Revolution. All dictators followed the same routine of torture, as if they had all read the same manual of sadistic etiquette. And now, in the humorous, friendly, happy-go-lucky land of Mark Twain, Doremus saw the homicidal maniacs having just as good a time as they had had in central Europe.

CHAPTER 30

Doremus Jessup: "I wonder which is worse?—the physical pain of being kicked, or the mental humiliation of being turned into a slave? Hell! Don't be sophistical! It's the pain in the behind that hurts most!"

CHAPTER 31

On Doremus and life in the concentration camp: The worst torture to Doremus, aside from the agony of actual floggings, was the waiting. The Waiting. It became a distinct, tangible thing, as individual and real as Bread or Water. How long would he be in? How long would he be in? Night and day, asleep and waking, he worried it, and by his bunk saw waiting the figure of Waiting, a gray, foul ghost. It was like waiting in a filthy station for a late train, not for hours but for months.

CHAPTER 36

Doremus Jessup: "More and more, as I think about history," he pondered, "I am convinced that everything that is worth while in the world has been accomplished by the free, inquiring, critical spirit, and that the preservation of this spirit is more important than any social system whatsoever. But the men of ritual and the men of barbarism are capable of shutting up the men of science and of silencing them forever."

CHAPTER 37

These rebels had most of them, before his election, believed in Buzz Windrip's fifteen points; believed that when he said he wanted to return the power pilfered by the bankers and the industrialists to the people, he more or less meant that he wanted to return the power of the bankers and industrialists to the people. As month by month they saw that they had been cheated with marked cards again, they were indignant; but they were busy with cornfield and sawmill and dairy and motor factory, and it took the impertinent idiocy of demanding that they march down into the desert and help steal a friendly country to jab them into awakening and into discovering that, while they had been asleep, they had been kidnaped by a small gang of criminals armed with high ideals, well-buttered words and a lot of machine guns. So profound was the revolt that the Catholic Archbishop of California and the radical Ex-Governor of Minnesota found themselves in the same faction.

CHAPTER 37
But there the revolt halted, because in the America, which had so warmly praised itself for its "widespread popular free education," there had been so very little education, widespread, popular, free, or anything else, that most people did not know what they wanted—indeed knew about so few things to want at all.

CHAPTER 38
So Doremus rode out, saluted by the meadow larks, and onward all day, to a hidden cabin in the Northern Woods where quiet men awaited news of freedom. And still Doremus goes on in the red sunrise, for a Doremus Jessup can never die.

The Prodigal Parents (1938)

The Prodigal Parents is more proof that Sinclair Lewis did, indeed, have the time machine constructed by H.G. Wells. Or, it's just further proof that the more things change, the more they stay the same. I will be the first to admit that I have a difficult time working with younger generations–I often find them spoiled and entitled. But when I read *The Prodigal Parents*, I ponder whether that has always been how older people view the younger set.

The Prodigal Parents takes place in the 1930's, well before the word 'Millennial' was ever used to describe a person. Fred and Hazel Cornplow have two children. Sara, the daughter, has recently graduated from college and lives at home. Howard, the son, is about to be a senior in high school. Fred and Hazel are good parents...and, that's the whole problem.

Mr. and Mrs. Cornplow have created a couple of monsters. Readers of this book most likely assume that I'm using 'monsters' in the figurative sense. I assure you; I am stating that the Cornplow children are literal monsters.

Howard and Sara, in their warped brains, have no understanding of consequence. They take advantage of their parents at every turn and seem to have no shame. Howard and Sara require money daily and worse, they feel so entitled to it that they assume it's theirs. When Mr. Cornplow finally does decide to cut back on their expenses, they attempt, nearly successfully, to have him committed to a mental hospital.

During a classic episode of Sinclair Lewisian role reversal, the parents run away from the kids–it's their only chance at sanity. They fully realize that it's their own fault–the children weren't simply born this way. They had been too good, too supportive, and too unwilling to see their kids face the pain of everyday life.

Today, we would call Fred and Hazel 'helicopter parents.' Perhaps there have always been helicopter and prodigal parents. Could it be that our society is so much more prosperous now that we see the products of these parents more often than we used to? My Grandma Francy used to say, "If your kids don't cry when they're kids, then you will cry when they're not." She was probably correct. However, as Sinclair Lewis would note, that sentiment is much easier said than corrected.

CHAPTER 2
Frederick William Cornplow on his son's latest car accident: "Grrrrr!" said Fred Wm. For this was the third calamitous accident Howard had achieved in two years, and each time Fred had determined that it was his duty, finally, to say 'Grrrrr!'

CHAPTER 3
Hazel Cornplow on her husband having a fever: "My! It does seem hot!" she exulted, with the pleasure all right-thinking persons feel in discovering that the best-beloved is helpless and that we shall be allowed to manage him.

CHAPTER 6
There is a vulgar error about rattlesnakes. Hordes of sensible people assume that it is treacherous in a rattlesnake to bite the tourists, but to himself a rattlesnake is an honest, kind-hearted family man who believes that human beings treacherously kill a lot more rattlesnakes than snakes kill humans.

CHAPTER 6
Fred Cornplow to his daughter: "Maybe you're not to blame personally. Whole country's full of smart young people whose folks have seen 'em to school and done all they could to help 'em socially and financially, and the kids despise 'em for being so soft, and don't for

one second hesitate to correct their parents' manners and historical dates!"

CHAPTER 9

Fred Cornplow: "Good Lord, son, I expect to help you get started. But only started. I don't expect to carry you for years and years, like a lot of parents are doing nowadays. I guess that's another demand the Youth Movement is making on Congress—let the old folks do it—penalize the folks that like to work by making 'em support the ones that don't."

CHAPTER 13

Fredk Wm., that man of mechanisms, usually drove, even in the city, and economize on time by taking fifteen minutes to find a parking space in order to avoid an eight-minute walk.

CHAPTER 18

Fred Cornplow: "What can a parent, that isn't more'n average bright himself, do for his children? Maybe leave them alone? If I only knew!...Maybe the poor, conceited little flute player loves his daughter, in his fool fashion. Wants to keep her...He's lost her. Do we always lose the people we love; only keep the people that we don't plague with loving? I guess those are the real wars—men against women—parents against children—and not all this monkey business in Europe. I'd like an armistice!"

CHAPTER 21

Fred Cornplow on finding several of his daughter's unpaid bills: "I won't pay one cent of 'em," he stormed—with twenty-five percent honesty.

CHAPTER 22

Hazel Cornplow on her daughter Sara: "I know, Fred, I know, but I also know how Sara is, and if she makes up her mind and starts nagging, we'll give in to her to save trouble. The only way you could handle it would be to run away from her."

CHAPTER 26

Fred Cornplow: "But isn't it the craziest doggone thing in this crazy world today, where half the nations are willing to go to war for the right to be slaves, that children have become the bossy parents, now, and the parents scared kids!"

CHAPTER 28

So, for Fredk Wm, his home was turned into a house; and a house was easier to leave than was a home.

CHAPTER 31

There is no way in which a normally stubborn husband can more fruitfully surprise and annoy his loved ones than being a 'good patient', which means a man who brightly agrees with the family doctor even when the doctor isn't sure that he agrees with himself.

CHAPTER 34

Fred Cornplow on traveling to Europe: "You'd be surprised, but they sell clothes in Europe, too. And I'll bet anything, maybe you could buy toothbrushes there."

CHAPTER 36

It made his voyage of discovery of himself curiously easier to travel with a pleasant person who did not embarrass him by understanding him.

CHAPTER 38

Annabel Cornplow on Fred and Hazel believing that their trip to Europe caused their children's issues: "No. Your going isn't to blame. But maybe your putting it off so long is. Sara and Howard thought you'd always be there and nurse them."

CHAPTER 40

Fred Cornplow: "If seems to me now that it isn't going where you want to that is freedom, but knowing that you can go."

Bethel Merriday (1940)

If all of Sinclair Lewis's novels came to life, and if I were heterosexual, I would be madly in love with Bethel Merriday. (Incidentally, the odds of Lewis novels coming to life are better than the odds of me becoming heterosexual.) Bethel Merriday is perfect: She's smart, quick-witted, deeply committed to her own happiness, and she's strong. Bethel is another of Sinclair Lewis's strong career women. However, unlike Ann Vickers, Bethel has no idea of the strength she contains. It's the ignorance of this knowledge that is, ironically, Bethel's strongest trait. (I'll marry Bethel Merriday and Ann Vickers will be my best friend...yeah...that will work well.)

Bethel Merriday is a book about the American theatre. Sinclair Lewis was no stranger to the stage. His official Broadway credits include producer of one play and playwright of three others. In addition to Broadway, he produced, directed, and even acted in several regional productions based on his writing. From reading *Bethel Merriday*, it's clear that while working in the theatre, Lewis must have immersed himself in every aspect of production.

All theatrical roles, both onstage and backstage, are on full display. The politics of this highly collaborative art form take much of the attention away from the actual show—just like real life. The divas, the wealthy producers, the gorgeous leading men, the hopeful understudies, the dictating directors, and the inconsistent audiences all star in this story.

Among all this action is Bethel Merriday. She's a young and hopeful dreamer from a small New England town. Throughout the novel she literally finds her voice as she travels around the country. It's so easy to fall in love with her that I physically cringe whenever something unfortunate occurs in her life. And, I'm not alone—multiple men propose marriage to her in the novel, some of them at the same time. Bethel truly loves the theatre. People naturally flock to those who love their job, mostly because those who love their job love their life.

Above all, *Bethel Merriday* is a story about hard work. Very hard work. American history likes us to believe that the only people who work hard are farmers, teachers, soldiers, and anyone who worked in a factory before 1978. We are mostly ignorant to the work of art. Bethel is up early and never retires until well after the audience has left at the end of the evening. The hours required to memorize the words of Shakespeare alone are a full-time job. Add to that the hours of painting, sewing, managing personalities, lifting box after box of whatever, bookkeeping, advertising, and just plain living.

I love that there was a time, before instant celebrity, when hard work was rewarded. I love that Sinclair Lewis understood the importance of theatre just as he did the importance of medicine. I also love Bethel Merriday.

CHAPTER 1

Five months after the six-year-old Bethel gave her imitation of the old lady, the Black Shirts marched bravely into the maws of the movie cameras in Rome; and five months after that, Hitler bounded out of a Munich beer garden. But perhaps it was as important that at this time John Barrymore was playing *Hamlet* and Pauline Lord *Anna Christie* and the Theatre Guild producing *Back to Methuselah*. They were so much less stagy.

CHAPTER 1

The Rex, a drugstore which was less of a drugstore than a bookstore, less of a bookstore than a cigar store, less of a cigar store than a restaurant, was characteristic of a somewhat confused purpose in American institutions, whereby the government has been a producer of plays and motion pictures, movie producers are owners of racing stables, churches are gymnasiums and dance halls, telegraph offices are agencies for flowers and tickets, authors are radio comedians, aviators are authors, and the noblest purpose of newspapers is to publish photographs of bathing girls.

CHAPTER 5

Valentine sat down facing the back of a wooden chair. And that was the first time, outside of the movies, that Bethel had ever seen this posture, and she noted and put away the fact that it made his fat knees prominent and very silly.

CHAPTER 7

How many more times would she find that she had graduated only into new freshmanhood? Freshman as a baby, freshman in her first year in grammar school, freshman in high school, freshman in college, freshman in a summer theatre, freshman on the professional stage—perhaps freshman in marriage and freshman as a star—would it end only with the death and her awakening to freshmanhood in heaven?

CHAPTER 11

Bethel was not yet aware of the basic rule of the theatre that if you ever act with anyone, you will act with him again; that if you play St. Clair's daughter in *Uncle Tom's Cabin* under canvas on the Dakota circuit in 1893, you must not be surprised to find yourself cast as St. Clair's mother in a Gotham Theatre Alliance comedy by Molnar in 1940, with one of the original walk-on bloodhounds now advanced to a Pekingese in the boudoir scene.

CHAPTER 14

The whole business of rehearsal had an exasperated fascination. She had early noted that the actors who had the fewest lines were those who were least likely to be ready for entrance, and that the less they had to memorize the less likely they were to know it.

CHAPTER 14

But the moment came, the last day, when you weren't saying lines, weren't rehearsing, but playing, lost, absorbed, and that was the second when you left the earth and were flying.

CHAPTER 18

On Bethel's first New York apartment: Everything conceivable to the genius of American gadgetry was here, but reduced below tolerable human size, and fitted together without six square inches of the waste space that could be used only for walking, relaxing, dreaming or any other merely human need: bed, reading lamp and bedside table, upholstered arm-chair, combination bookcase and desk and radio and bureau, and a dressing-table so elegant that in the advertisements it would be referred to as 'milady's'. And a bathroom. It was nearly possible to sit in the tub and reach out and write a letter, open the hall door, open the window or answer the telephone.

CHAPTER 19

Mrs. Boyle was one of the highly competent English actors who, after working up a hatred for everything British, including fish and chips and the royal family, had come over to America chiefly because they could hate everything in these gangster-infested jungles even more.

CHAPTER 21

Bethel understood better now the improbable stories of understudies who prayed that their principals would fall through a trap door.

CHAPTER 21

And once, rather rudely, Zed invited her to dinner at an Italian restaurant in the East Forties, so far over that it was practically in Italy.

CHAPTER 24

Mahala to Bethel: "And the audience aren't good neighbors here, like a summer theatre, that are pulling for you to succeed. These are wolves. They want their two dollars and eighty cents' worth."

CHAPTER 25

She had never made a quantitative analysis of the relationship of ivy to education, but from observation of Point Royal to Yale, she had concluded that it was direct.

CHAPTER 27

Andy Deacon: "Everybody told me that all the farmers for sixty miles around would leap in their Fords and drive through blizzards to see *Romeo Meets Juliet*. Well, either they got sand in their carburettors or they preferred to stay home and listen to the radio, and maybe they're right."

CHAPTER 28

Then her nap, curled snugly on that heavenly bed. (The mattress was astonishingly named the Slumber Coaxie, and had, it seems, been Scientifically Constructed in accordance with the findings of a Conference of Forty Professors, Housewives and Social Leaders. But it really was a good mattress, once you got to sleep and forgot the lush poetry.)

CHAPTER 31

On an understudy taking over a role: He did fairly well, though he had never rehearsed the speech. He left out the line "From ancient grudge break to new mutiny", but apparently no one noticed. Certainly there was no sound of new mutiny breaking, out there in the awesome dark majesty of the audience.

CHAPTER 32

On Bethel encountering a sad colleague, Iris: When she saw Iris on Saturday evening, saw the soreness of tears in the corners of her eyes, Bethel herself wanted to cry, and swore a great vow that she could never again hate any woman...not even Mahala...much.

CHAPTER 33

On Bethel as Lady Capulet: She had been alive and competent as Lady Capulet; no amateurishness and no languishing. She had merited the good hand at the curtain call. But she never would know that the 'spontaneous applause' on her first exit had been about as spontaneous as a department-store Santa Claus. Doc Keezer, as he had done a hundred times on half a hundred tours, had been kneeling way down left, just behind the tormentor, and at her exit had given one mighty smack of his hands. That had started the clapping of the innocent audience for the innocent Bethel, and everybody had been very happy about it, including Doc.

CHAPTER 33

It is a fable that the 'fourth wall' of the stage is empty. There, massed, are the most influential part of the cast: the audience. On their acting, their timing, their professional training, depends the contributory vividness of the rest of the cast. And audiences differ, from night to night, at least as much as individual actors. An untrained audience is an uncomfortable a collaborator as an untrained surgeon or an untrained lover.

Gideon Planish (1943)

Gideon Planish is proof that Sinclair Lewis was an equal opportunity satirizer. If *Elmer Gantry* and *It Can't Happen Here* are aimed at the conservative fundamentalists, then *Gideon Planish* is aimed at their radical liberal counterparts. It's clear that Lewis found plenty of fault on both ends of the political spectrum. I wonder how he would fare in our modern polarized world.

In many regards, *Gideon Planish* is a direct accompaniment to *Elmer Gantry*. In fact, Elmer Gantry himself is a minor character in *Gideon Planish*. We learn that the good reverend, having left Winnemac, is now a radio preacher in New York City. Lewis doesn't let us know if his wife and children are still around, but we do get to meet his young and beautiful secretary.

If a young Gideon Planish would have discovered religion instead of education, he could just as easily have been another Elmer Gantry (and, vice-versa.) But as it is, Gideon rises through the ranks of higher education until he enters the world of philanthropic activism. His journey takes him around the Midwest until he finally hits the corrupt world of organized foundations in New York City.

Gideon Planish is, of course, from Winnemac. However, we discover that he's not from Zenith. Mr. Planish grew up in Vulcan, the seventh largest city in the state. He spends some time in the Winnemac capital of Galop de Vache and, in this novel, we get a better description of that city.

Overall, *Gideon Planish* isn't as well written as *Elmer Gantry*. I really wish it was because the premise of this book is brilliant. Alas, Lewis wrote *Gideon Planish* at a time when he wasn't in full control of his satirical powers. Still, there are some fascinating developments in the novel, and we do get to know Gideon quite well.

The characters of Gideon Planish and Elmer Gantry are unequal as well–and that's a good thing. Reverend Gantry never shows remorse and continues to take advantage of people's religious insecurities. In contrast, Gideon Planish does question his actions and seems to have a desire for liberal organizations to keep a few of their smaller promises.

CHAPTER 1
Gideon Planish's first oratory: "It seems to me, what this country needs is young men in politics that have higher standards of honesty and more profound knowledge of history and, uh, well, of civics than the politicians of today, and who will advance the unfinished work lying before us of leading this country to uh, higher standards of Freedom, Liberty, Equality, Fraternity, Freedom, and–well, I mean higher standards of–."

CHAPTER 3
As he was often to do in his later career as a professional promoter of ideas, Gid nearly convinced himself of the truth of his own crusade.

CHAPTER 4
Gideon Planish: "I'm still more tempted by politics than by anything else. I tell you, politics needs men with intellectual training. I could be a doctor, but I don't like sick people. Or a lawyer, but I hate sticking in an office. Or a clergyman. Yes, I been a lot tempted by the ministry. But I do like a glass of beer now and then, and anyway, I don't know as I could work up the real feeling of instant communion with God that I'd like to, if I was going to go around doing a lot of public praying. So, you see, I do really feel a call to politics."

CHAPTER 5
Dr. Edith Minton: "Oh, I've just had an afternoon of girl freshmen who couldn't make up their minds whether they wanted to be scholars or women or have careers."

Main Speak: Quotes from the Work of Sinclair Lewis

CHAPTER 7

For a gentleman professor in Kinnikinick College to look upon a maiden student as a human being was poorly thought of, and to meet her over a dish of marshmallow, ground nuts, caramel and two kinds of ice cream was as dangerous morally as it was dietetically.

CHAPTER 9

Professor Planish did have two brothers and a sister, but since he had left home they had existed for him only as a theory.

CHAPTER 10

Peony Planish: "I hate to spend money, and I hate to be in debt—I just hate it. It's simply that I like to *have* things, don't you see?"

CHAPTER 10

Mabel Grove had, as happens in the Middlewest, leaped from crossroad hamlet to small city without ever having had the leisure to stop and be merely a pleasant village. It had concrete paving, a seven-story office-building belonging to a bank, and a dozen rather squashed apartment houses. By 1940 it would also have a radio station, a chromium cocktail bar, a public swimming pool, and a much-mentioned unmentionable scandal about a male high-school teacher. It showed that in eighty years the prairies can to as far as Europe in eight hundred.

CHAPTER 10

They talked of taxes. Dean Planish hadn't known there were so many kinds of taxes: federal and state and county and city, road and improvement and amusement, licenses to sell tobacco and to sell pop. They talked of the congressional candidates for this fall, and they talked of caucuses. The Dean had always assumed that he knew what a caucus was, just as he assumed that he knew what an aardvark was, but suddenly he wasn't sure that he knew how either of them looked.

CHAPTER 14

Before the annual conference of the Heskett Foundation, Dr. Planish had learned everything about it except why it existed at all. The two mysteries regarding any organization for philanthropy are who really owns it and what, if anything, it actually does, besides creates a pretty letterhead and provide a warm office for the chief executive to take naps in.

CHAPTER 19

There is a particular flavor to Celebrities, to people who have their names in the papers and who expect to be recognized on the street. Most of them will, within a year or two, slide back into the pit of anonymity whence they scrambled, and that will either make them human again or, in their resentment, destroy them utterly, for a Celebrity who has lost celebrity is the emptiest of God's curios.

CHAPTER 21

The liberal churches were turning into lecture halls, but in 1930—as would later be true in 1940, and probably in 1960—the solid Fundamentalists, who knew that God created the world in six days and has spent His time since then in intensely disliking it, still held the true faith unshaken.

CHAPTER 22

One of the mysteries is the origin of dirty stories and political anecdotes. A tale will be repeated ten million times over ten years, and yet the original author, honest fellow, will be unknown, unhonored.

CHAPTER 25

Deacon Wheyfish on philanthropy: "What can a man purchase in the way of a motor car, a bathtub or a radio that will afford him such spiritual benefit, or for that matter such keen pride and pleasure and social prestige, as the knowledge that he is permitting the better organization executives the means and the leisure to go around doing good, and the reputation of being the best giver in his whole neighborhood? We may have to hypnotize him a little to make him realize that, but how satisfied he will be when he does! You bet!"

Main Speak: Quotes from the Work of Sinclair Lewis

CHAPTER 25

Deacon Wheyfish: "Don't forget that the menace of war, properly presented, will scare into giving even those people, rich or poor, who have been the most obdurate to our pitiful appeals for help."

CHAPTER 29

Reverend Gantry on World War Two: In his sermon, the Reverend said that Europe was at war because people, particularly in this section of New York, did not go to church more regularly. He and God were displeased.

CHAPTER 31

It is not Broadway that is the Main Street of New York, but the long, thin, prandial Speakers' Table, and every familiar—too, too familiar—face along it knows intimately and detests furiously all the other inevitable and self-opening faces there.

CHAPTER 32

Unknown Train Passenger: "I decided that the rule was that if an organization was set up to achieve one definite social end, it was virtuous, but if it was started by one busybody who just wanted a career and a salary, it was bad. But that's a simple-minded rule. Look at the Anti-Saloon League. I suppose it did have a lot of good intentions as well as an awful lot of millions, and look at the way it made the idea of temperance ridiculous for another hundred years. In a republic like this, I'm scared of *any* private organization that can spend thousands on propaganda—that can persuade thousands of people to telegraph their congressman to do what the private organization demands. It's a little too much like a private army—like the Brown Shirts."

CHAPTER 32

(Note: The following passage is a bit long for a quote, however, it is quite profound and deserves to be recorded here.)

After he came back to New York, Dr. Planish made a lot of speeches, and there was a quiet man who heard one of them, and this quiet man got to thinking.

He thought that the one thing that might break down American Democracy was the hysterical efficiency with which these pressure groups crusaded to seize all the benefits of that Democracy for themselves; the farm bloc, the women's bloc, the manufacturer's associations, the Protestant ministerial associations, the labor unions, the anti-labor unions, the Communist Party and the Patriotic Flag Associations. Drug stores combining to force legislation forbidding the sale of aspirin on trains. Irish Catholics voting not as Americans but as Irish *and* Catholics, Swedish Lutherans voting as Swedish Lutherans, Arkansas Baptists noting as Neanderthals.

Catholics forbidding the Episcopalians to advance birth-control, and Methodists forbidding the Unitarians to drink their ancestral rum, and people who really believe in Christianity overwhelmingly outvoted by all these monopolies.

Gangs of Fascists damning the Jews—always the opening gambit in any mass insanity—until the Jews are forced to create their own alliances, and these become a new Sanhedrin that censors the Jews who won't submit to the new Mosaic Law.

The Friends of Russia, the Friends of Germany, the Friends of the British Empire, the Friends of the Slovenes and Croats, the Sons of the American Revolution, and the Sons of Dog Fanciers.

Each of these private armies led by devout fanatics—not always on salary—who believe that the way to ensure freedom for everybody is to shut up every one of their opponents in jail for life, and that this is a very fine, new solution.

God save poor America, this quiet man thought, from all the zealous and the professionally idealistic, from eloquent women and generous sponsors and administrative ex-preachers and natural-born Leaders and Napoleonic newspaper executives and all people who like to make long telephone calls and write inspirational memoranda.

Cass Timberlane: A Novel of Husbands and Wives (1945)

Of all the novels of Sinclair Lewis, *Cass Timberlane* is the most difficult for me to understand. This is, as Lewis writes in the subtitle, a novel about husbands and wives. I, a man who has been married to another man for over twelve years, find it hard to relate to many of the situations presented in the book. While reading *Cass Timberlane* I can't help but wonder how any heterosexual couple manages to stay together. With that said, this novel is infinitely better than modern comedians with their jokes of mothers-in-law and the position of toilet seats.

Cass Timberlane is a divorced middle-aged man living in Grand Republic, Minnesota. He is an elected judge on the Radisson County court and a former US Congressman. He is an accomplished person. His life changes when Jinny, a much younger free spirit, takes the witness stand during a trial over which he is presiding. He pretty much falls instantly in love with her and so begins the tale.

Cass Timberlane takes place in another of Lewis's fictional Midwestern towns: Grand Republic, Minnesota. Grand Republic is significantly larger than Gopher Prairie, but significantly smaller than Zenith, Winnemac. I've lived in Grand Republics before; they were called St. Cloud, Duluth, and Rochester. In all cases, these midsize municipalities have all the problems of small towns and large cities without the benefits of either one.

Readers may want to believe that Lewis drew upon his two failed marriages as the inspiration for *Cass Timberlane*. Obviously, he does; however, Jinny, the female subject, cannot possibly be based on either of his wives. Sinclair Lewis's first wife, Grace Heggar, was a professional in the publishing field. His second wife was the acclaimed journalist Dorothy Thompson. In this novel, Jinny is neither of those things—she is not one of Lewis's stronger female characters.

Lewis interrupts the narrative of Cass and Jinny several times. He does this by presenting stories titled "An Assemblage of Husbands and Wives". These stories occur as separate stand-alone Chapters—they are all complete short stories. Sometimes humorous, sometimes profound, and sometimes downright tragic, these short stories define the genre of realism. Lewis shows exactly what has been occurring behind all those locked doors in Grand Republic. Nothing is left off the table, and it's somewhat striking to discover oneself within "An Assemblage of Husbands and Wives".

Cass Timberlane was published in 1945. I can't imagine a time when the US concept of marriage went through more change. The legalization of same-sex marriage is nothing compared to the social awareness that women were actually people. Lewis was born just twenty years after the Civil War. In a way, *Cass Timberlane* is a tribute to the pioneers of modern marriage. Without the social rules of the 19th Century, people just didn't know how to be married. This novel displays Sinclair Lewis's absolute fascination with this societal shift.

CHAPTER 1

Cass Timberlane on dating after divorce: "I guess that's the trouble. I apparently want someone who's so intelligent that she'll think I'm stupid, so independent that she'll never need me, so gay and daring that she'll think I'm slow. That's my pattern."

CHAPTER 2

On Grand Republic, Minnesota: It is large enough to have a Renoir, a school-system scandal, several millionaires, and a slum.

Main Speak: Quotes from the Work of Sinclair Lewis

CHAPTER 2

Grand Republic grew rich two generations ago through the uncouth robbery of forests, iron mines, and soil for wheat. With these almost exhausted, it rests in leafy quiet, wondering whether to become a ghost town or a living city. The Chamber of Commerce says that it has already became a city, but, in secret places where the two bankers on the school board cannot hear them, the better schoolteachers deny this.

CHAPTER 2

It is understood that the newer psychiatrists, like the older poets, believe that patients do fall in love at first sight.

CHAPTER 3

Dr. Drover on Eleanor Roosevelt: "The wife of President Franklin D. Roosevelt, a woman who has so betrayed her own class that she believes that miners and Negroes and women are American citizens, ought to be compelled by law to stay home."

CHAPTER 10

The surprising objects that you see when you leave your own Grand Republic and go traveling—pink snakes and polar bears—are nothing beside what you find when you stay at home and have a new girl and meet her friends, whose resentment of you is only less than your amazement that there are such people and that she likes them.

An Assemblage of Husbands and Wives: The Zebra Sisters

On Zoe Zebra's husband Harold: None of them was eccentric, except that Harold W. Wittick—just for a josh, everybody said; to show off and try to be different—asserted that he had once voted for a Democratic candidate for the presidency, Mr. Franklin Delano Roosevelt.

CHAPTER 14

Cass Timberlane, on Jinny: "I think I'm a good deal in love with her. I agree with you in saying 'damn her'! I didn't want to be in an earthquake. You're dead right, my dear, I do prefer quiet. But I'm simply God-smitten."

CHAPTER 15

Jinny, on the lack of people who travel: "But why is it that nobody ever does do any of the things that he's free to do?"

CHAPTER 16

Everybody in town—it being understood that everybody-in-town includes some three hundred persons out of the 85,000—discussed Jinny by telephone, by letter, over the directors' table, or at the Paul Bunyan Bar.

CHAPTER 18

Jinny: "I'll be all ready. Seven sharp." Which, in Jinny's time-schedule, meant ten minutes past seven, not very sharp.

CHAPTER 19

On winter in Minnesota: With November, the first snows had brought shouting cheerfulness to children with sleighs and blasphemy to drivers trying to slide their cars up the slippery roads to Ottawa Heights.

CHAPTER 20

Cass Timberlane: "Marriage and the common cold—the two persistent problems of mankind and the ones that have never been solved."

CHAPTER 20

Cass on Jinny: "One thing I do get clear about her. She is one of those extraordinary people who are not willing to settle down and wait for death, willing to play cards and yawn and gossip and actually speak of 'killing time,' when we have so little time. What life she has she will always live."

An Assemblage of Husbands and Wives: Gillian Brown–Violet Crenway

Gillian Brown was a business woman, a career woman, but she was human, and she had decided that for such a premature phenomenon as herself, there were but five matrimonial choices: to marry a man who was her superior and who would either cheat her or leave her flat, to marry an inferior whom she would pet and despise, to marry an equal, which would happen only by a miracle comparable to Jonah and his also undependable marine companion, to lie unwed and rigid, or to have company. She had tried all five.

CHAPTER 24

They fished again in the salt inlet, next day; they delightedly though erroneously believed that they saw a barracuda, a threatening moccasin; they felt valiant as only tourists can.

CHAPTER 26

If the world of the twentieth century, he vowed, cannot succeed in this one thing, married love, then it has committed suicide, all but the last moan, and whether Germany and France can live as neighbors is insignificant compared with whether Johann and Maria or Jean and Marie can live as lovers.

An Assemblage of Husbands and Wives: Benjamin and Petal Hearth

On Benjamin Hearth realizing that his wife was an alcoholic: He knew now. Yet such was his love for this woman, who was so refined and superior, that he would not permit himself to know what he knew.

CHAPTER 30

The true American is active even in his inactivities.

CHAPTER 33

On Jinny shopping in New York City: She yearned over furs and Irish linens and perfume-bottles with gold crowns for stoppers and folding card-tables so sturdy that you could sit on them—the clerk enthusiastically proved it. (He was fired for it, that evening; the table might have collapsed.) But there was a hard shrewdness in her, and she bought only one percent of the things that she would die if she did not have.

CHAPTER 36

Jinny on her illness: "So then I quit being so sorry for myself. I'd been feeling as if I were set aside from all normal people, as if I were a condemned man, with no hope. But after I'd talked to Mrs. Purdwin I got thinking about people that are really up against it: men without jobs in cities, farmers with mortgages and the crop has failed again and the kids are hungry and cold; all the awful things that we first-class passengers never know."

CHAPTER 39

Their autumn season of quarrels was to Cass as devastating and as senseless as a thunderstorm.

CHAPTER 41

As much as Cass, the reticent Jinny was offended by indecencies, yet she did see that it was demoralizingly funny when the embarrassed young Cass came in expectantly and had to be told that he and his poetic ardor were barred by the lunar rhythm.

CHAPTER 50

Cass Timberlane: "We're so civilized now that we can kill our horrid enemies—year-old children—two hundred miles away, but nobody except a few rather loveless professors has even begun to understand love."

CHAPTER 50

Cass Timberlane: "You cannot heal the problems of any one marriage until you heal the problems of an entire civilization founded upon suspicion and superstition; and you cannot heal the problems of a civilization thus founded until it realizes its own barbaric nature, and realizes that what it thought was brave was only cruel, what it thought was holy was only meanness, and what it thought Success was merely the paper helmet of a clown more nimble than his fellows, scrambling for a peanut in the dust of an ignoble circus."

CHAPTER 51

Jinny: "I guess that after being lost in these Eastern crowds, so indifferent, I want to go some place where they love you enough to hate you if you don't love *them*."

Kingsblood Royal (1947)

Sometimes Sinclair Lewis's greatness works against him. His most famous novels are often, and incorrectly, considered unapproachable for high school students. Consequently, his entire work is neglected by literature teachers. This is quite unfortunate because *Kingsblood Royal* is absolutely riveting and should be read as part of a modern American Literature curriculum.

Kingsblood Royal is not a typical Sinclair Lewis satire. While there are some satirical elements found in the book, the story of Neil Kingsblood is too terrifying to be completely satirical. This book makes me angry. Very, very angry.

Neil Kingsblood lives with his wife in Grand Republic, Minnesota. It's the same Grand Republic of *Cass Timberlane* and Judge Timberlane makes several appearances throughout *Kingsblood Royal*. (I won't divulge if Jinny makes any appearances in *Kingsblood Royal* because that will spoil the end of *Cass Timberlane* for intuitive readers.)

Neil goes through life as any normal white American did in 1944: He's successful, admired, extremely handsome, and fairly racist. His wife, Vestal, is even more racist, as are pretty much all their family and friends. But then a horrifying truth is revealed when Neil discovers that his mother is part Negro. (Negro is the term used in the novel as it was written in 1947. Also, be advised that because *Kingsblood Royal* is meant to be an accurate description of race relations in the 1940's, the other n-word is used frequently.)

What is a typical white banker like Neil supposed to do with this information? Today, we wouldn't think much of it. But in 1944 Minnesota, having any Negro ancestor—no matter how

distant–meant that all subsequent generations were 100%
Negro. Neil will lose his job. He's broken the law by marrying
a white woman. His daughter could be kicked out of school.
His parents and siblings will be ruined. He'll surely, and legally,
lose his house. And, unfortunately, lynching did still occur in
Minnesota at that time.

The terror in *Kingsblood Royal* comes from the quite apparent realism that whatever is happening to Neil could just as
easily happen to any of us. None of his problems are his fault,
but they are his problems nonetheless. In true Sinclair Lewis
style, nothing is sugar-coated in this book. It's full of violence,
graphic bigotry, heart-wrenching anxiety, and the bullying of
children. This novel does not make me proud of Minnesota.

I've mentioned earlier that Sinclair Lewis wrote strong females into many of his books. Of all the heroic and modern
women of Sinclair Lewis, Vestal Kingsblood just might be my
favorite. She grows and changes amidst unspeakable adver-
sity. The last paragraph of *Kingsblood Royal* belongs to her–it's
simply magnificent. (I have not included any portion of this
paragraph here in order to preserve a future reader's discovery.)

CHAPTER 1

The Bilinghams, who knew that the true center of the solar system is the corner of Fifth Avenue and Fifty-seventh Street, would have
been irritated to find out how many of the simpletons in the valley
below them believed that New York contained nothing but hotels,
burlesque shows, a ghetto and Wall Street.

CHAPTER 2

Mr. William Stopple (and remember that not long ago he was
mayor of Grand Republic) privately advises you that Sylvan Park is just
as free of Jews, Italians, Negroes, and the exasperatingly poor as it is
of noise, mosquitoes, and rectangularity of streets.

CHAPTER 3

The struggle of the honest and innocent Neil to express his racial ideas was complicated by the fact that he had no notion what these ideas were.

CHAPTER 4

On Vestal's ignorance of minority populations and their religions: She perceived that she had been assuming that Christmas was a holiday invented by the Pilgrim Fathers at Plymouth, along with Santa Claus and yule-logs and probably the winter solstice, and must all be delightful novelties to persons of African decent.

CHAPTER 13

Neil Kingsblood on realizing that his daughter shares his ancestors: "All right. If Bid is a Negro, then everything I've ever heard about Negroes–yes, and maybe everything I've heard about the Jews and the Japs and the Russians, about religion and politics–all of that may be a lie, too.

CHAPTER 15

Not till he had almost reached home did it occur to him that his twenty-eight hours as a Negro was possibly too brief a training for him to take over all of his people's manners.

CHAPTER 16

On Neil Kingsblood meeting Dr. Ash: He was, in fact, deciding, "This Davis is a bright-looking fellow. I didn't know there were any Negroes like him. Well, how could I? I've never even had the chance to see them." (As a matter of fact, a few months before, Neil had sat opposite Dr. Ash Davis in a bus, had heard him talking to a large Negro with a clerical collar, and had never looked at either of them.)

CHAPTER 19

Emerson Woolcape, on Mrs. Woolcape stating that she doesn't mind the terms 'Negro' and 'colored person': "What Mother means," Emerson explained, "is that we dislike both terms intensely, but we consider them slightly less ruffling than 'nigger' or 'coon' or 'jig' or 'spade' or 'smoke' or any of the other labels by which white ditch-diggers indicate their superiority to Negro bishops. We expect it to take a few more decades before we're simply called 'Americans' or 'human beings.'"

CHAPTER 19
Mrs. Woolcape: "That child is just beginning to learn the humiliation that every Negro feels every day, particularly in our self-satisfied North Middlewest. In the South, we're told we're dogs who simply have to get used to our kennels, and then we'll get a nice bone and a kind word. But up here we're told that we're complete human beings, and encouraged to hope and think, and as a consequence we feel the incessant little reminders of supposed inferiority, the careless humiliations, more than our Southern cousins do the fear of lynching."

CHAPTER 20
He found that Mary Woolcape carried out the myth of the "typical Negress" in one detail: she was an excellent cook. But he was still novice enough to marvel that they did not have fried chicken and watermelon for Sunday dinner, but a quite Aryan roast of beef.

CHAPTER 21
Neil Kingsblood: "This could be me. They have lynched Negroes, even in Minnesota. They would hate me even more than they do fellows that have always been colored. I could feel that rope."

CHAPTER 23
Dr. Davis: "Captain Kingsblood, it isn't only the humiliation of segregation that riles us. It's the impossibility of telling when the simplest thing, like raising your hat to a nun, will be considered criminal, and you'll get slugged for it. It's that doubt that makes so many timid fellows go grab a razor."

CHAPTER 25
Dr. Davis: "I'll promise to keep off the race-talk, though there no complete cure for it. The other day, in the bathroom, I read a label of 'facial tissues' as 'racial issues.'"

Main Speak: Quotes from the Work of Sinclair Lewis

CHAPTER 28

On dinner with Rod Aldwick, a bigoted attorney: At dinner, Rod volunteered his plans for the whole future of his son, Graham, aged nine but already doomed. Graham would, like his father, go to Lawrenceville with a couple of summers at Culver Military Academy, go joyfully on to Princeton and Harvard Law, enter his father's firm, enter the National Guard, be a gentleman, marry a lady and, when his time came, defend Anglo-American Civilization and the Bar Association against Spigs, Wops, Kikes, Chinks, Bolos, and the Pan-Islamic Union.

CHAPTER 35

It was tacitly understood by the whole family that he was to say nothing *until*. Just when *until* would arrive had not been mentioned.

CHAPTER 35

Show was falling all day, and from time to time somebody would say brightly, "Fine! It's a real *white* Christmas," and every time he heard it, Neil thought, "So even Christmas gets jimcrowed."

CHAPTER 38

Unknown woman: "My young nigger friend, do you know what God is going to do to you for having set yourself up against His plain commandment that Ethiopia shall stay in perpetual bondage in the kitchen and not go riding in no public buses with no decent white folks? Oh, he that heedeth not the words of God, he shall go down to hell and gnashing, and that's the Bible-truth, that's God's truth, praise His merciful name!"

CHAPTER 38

Mr. Prutt: "As a born Yankee, I have always had great commiseration for you colored people, and have always maintained that it would be more charitable not to educate you beyond the fourth grade, so that you will not get false ideas and realize how unhappy you are."

CHAPTER 43

Then they sold the car. In the United States, that is the same as saying, "Then they sold their four daughters into slavery."

CHAPTER 45

He had not known that to a great many people job-hunting was a heavier part of life than job-holding; more nervous, more humiliating and entirely unpaid.

CHAPTER 49

Vestal Kingsblood: "That's the trouble! I've been brought up to believe that darkies are funny people, dancing and laughing and saying, 'Oh, thank you, Miss Vestal, ma'am, you white folks is sure wonderful to us poor coons.' But this David sketch thinks I'm just another female that's dumb about chemistry and economics."

The God-Seeker (1949)

The God-Seeker is a complete departure from the writing style that Sinclair Lewis perfected. But since *The God-Seeker* is pretty much perfect, we can deduce that Lewis was a writer capable of exploring multiple genres. Many people, including history buffs, are surprised to learn that Sinclair Lewis wrote a book about the history of Minnesota. As a life-long Minnesotan, reading *The God-Seeker* makes me wonder why I didn't learn any of this in high school. (Do you mean to tell me, Sinclair Lewis, that Goodhue was an actual person? I thought Goodhue was just the name of a county that gets blizzard warnings on the television from time to time.)

The God-Seeker is historical fiction at its finest. The hero of the story is a young want-to-be missionary from New England named Aaron Gadd. Aaron is my biggest Sinclair Lewis male crush and would make a much better mate for me than Elmer Gantry. He makes the perilous journey to 1848 rural Minnesota, just one year before the Territory of Minnesota was officially declared.

Sinclair Lewis does not sugar-coat any of the often-horrible history. (Perhaps that's why I didn't learn about these events in school.) At the time, in this desolate land, several factions were fighting for control of the would-be economy. Fur-traders, early politicians, transportation moguls, and missionaries themselves all wanted a piece of the pie. A pie, incidentally, that didn't belong to them.

The plight of Minnesota's native populations is the main storyline of *The God-Seeker*. The situation is complex as the Dakota and Chippewa frequently war with each other. At the

Michael Fridgen

same time, the various denominations of missionaries can't get along either. There are a lot of people fighting with each other in this novel. The situation is complicated further when Mother Nature throws her hat in the ring in the form of blizzards, wild animals, and disease.

While the main storyline is the treatment of Native Americans, the main *theme* is general theology. Aaron Gadd navigates the murky waters of Christian missionary philosophy. Would Jesus approve of these ruthless crusaders? Aaron's inability to refrain from questioning his dogma leads to a host of trouble.

The God-Seeker is long in scope. We see the fledgling villages of Pig's Eye and St. Anthony grow into the proper cities of St. Paul and Minneapolis. And, eventually, Minnesota joins the United States in 1858.

While this work is historical fiction, don't assume that Sinclair Lewis's distinctive voice is absent. He is, indeed, quite present in *The God-Seeker*. His views on organized religion are fully evident—as is his disgust for the bigotry against Native Americans and escaped Black slaves from the southern states. Lewis describes, well ahead of its time, the terrible fate of two young men who were more than just "special friends". (There wasn't even a word for such a thing in 1848—except, perhaps, sickness.)

Those of us who grew up in the Midwest often believe that all the tumultuous events of American History occurred on either the East Coast or the Wild, Wild West. *The God-Seeker* opened my eyes to my own past. Carol Kennicott's problems with Main Street are a direct result of Aaron Gadd's problems with the missionaries, which are a direct result of the problems fringe Protestants had in New England, which are a direct result of the religious intolerance of the British colonists that came to this land seeking religious freedom in the first place.

Main Speak: Quotes from the Work of Sinclair Lewis

CHAPTER 2

Hezrai Gadd: "Boy—Aaron, d' you say it was?—they's two kinds of fun in politics: revolution against tyrants, and then revolution against the revolutionists when *they* turn tyrants."

CHAPTER 4

Deacon Popplewood: "Well, Aary, I think it's all right for a Christian to do anything he wants to, providin' it ain't dancin' or whorin' or having truck with Unitarians or the Catholics," said the Deacon.

CHAPTER 6

He did not worry. He had been able to talk himself and drink himself out of his earlier fear that a just God and an angry God might suddenly become just and angry.

CHAPTER 11

The actual eating took less time than Mr. Harge's rather expostulatory grace-before-meat.

CHAPTER 12

Selene Lanark on being half-white and half-Dakota: "I'm clean flummoxed about it. Sometimes I love the whites—they're clever—and hate the Indians. Sometimes I love the Dakota, because they don't just grub for houses and carriages, and I wish I were more like that—clean of things. And sometimes I hate them both!"

CHAPTER 14

In the year 1848, when Aaron Gadd set out for Minnesota, he did not know that this frontier, for all its battles between Chippewa and Sioux, was a valley of peace compared with the culture that he was leaving: the hostilities of abolition, socialism, transcendentalism, women's rights, spiritualism, mesmerism, phrenology, vegetarianism, and the Millerites who believed that the world ought to have ended in 1843 and would make up for it right away.

CHAPTER 17

In front of the Chapel of St. Paul, founded by the brave Catholic padres and so artfully constructed of logs that it resembled a charming Gothic chapel reproduced in oak and from which softly rang the Angelus, strolling or taking the air in jingling carriages, passed and repressed the gay throngs: gold-laced soldiers swinging great sabres, bright-eyed ladies with silk parasols chattering coquettishly in a dozen melodious tongues, statuesque Sioux chiefs with jewel-adorned eagle-feather war-bonnets and fathomless eyes, watching the cheerful bustle of their white acquaintance, the flower of Minnay-Sotor or the Land of the Sky-blue Water.

CHAPTER 17

Unknown citizen of St. Paul: "Now we got a lawyer, we got civilization, which I understand to mean that a man has a chance to get rich without working."

CHAPTER 18

On Aaron Gadd passing a Sioux woman with an infant: "The baby eyed him back, and registered him as a decent-enough young man possibly worth an infant's philosophical study. That was in the fall of 1848. In 1949, that Indian baby is still alive, a retired grocer and a Civil War veteran, slightly over a hundred years old, still dwelling within sight of Lake Calhoun, in a twelve-story Minneapolis apartment house.

CHAPTER 24

Mercie Harge: "Missionary work is hard on the men, but it kills the women."

CHAPTER 24

Mercie Harge: "Missionaries like Harge are so powerful about not tippling or soiling the Lord's Day, but how they do love to make love, and the more uplifted they feel, the more affectionate they get. And there you are with another precious coming, and no doctor, and you're no longer a girl—even if you aren't but twenty-odd by the calendar.

Main Speak: Quotes from the Work of Sinclair Lewis

You're just a combination of scrub-woman and stock farm, and you're supposed to yell Hallelujah about it."

CHAPTER 26

Caesar Lanark: "The only difference between us is that you think all races are equally good, and I think they're all equally bad and slovenly and in need of being controlled by their superiors—by which, no doubt, I mean myself."

CHAPTER 28

Squire Harge: "If these heathen would devote that energy to fighting the wiles of Satan instead of running aimlessly with little sticks, we might build a Christian community here, like Scranton."

CHAPTER 31

Medicine Spider: "White women actually dress up to please their husbands, instead of, as is normal, the men showing off to please the women. And white men spend all their time inventing new ways of lighting, so that women can sit up and work half the night while the men snore."

CHAPTER 32

Squire Harge: "And the time is so short that we'll have the field to ourselves. Once these foreign cattle like the Irish Catholics and the German Lutherans and all the Scandinavians intrude here, the true theology, as handed down by the Presbyterians—and I suppose by the Congregationalists—will be adulterated, and the Indians won't know *what* to believe."

CHAPTER 36

On Aaron Gadd killing a deer: Medicine Spider forgave him for being an atheist with no belief in Taku-skan-skan not even in the Wakan Wohanpi feast by which a decent man returns thanks to the gods for their bounty. She told Black Wolf to explain that if Aaron would remain among the Dakota long enough and humbly learn how to share everything with others, how to listen to the spirits of animals and streams and winds, he might yet become a saved soul and a Man.

CHAPTER 37

Mercie Harge: "You can't have a real sunset unless there's a smell of coffee—real *coffee* coffee!"

CHAPTER 38

On Aaron Gadd noticing that Squire Harge was courting Huldah: He saw that Harge was ardent about Huldah, if it showed in nothing more than his way of handing her a hymn book. In 1848, a woman who had a hymn book handed to her like that was already compromised.

CHAPTER 39

The Squire lined it out, reading and expounding each sentence in English and then in Dakota—which he hoped to be Dakota, what he believed to be Dakota, but which the three astonished women did not seem to recognize as Dakota.

CHAPTER 40

The older people at the Mission considered Christmas a rather pagan feast and highly wasteful of food, but the children clamored after it.

CHAPTER 41

Black Wolf on the Christian doctrine: "Among their demigods are Santa Claus, Luck (whom they worship by striking wood), saints, angels, seraphs, witches, fairies, vampires, evil spirits, the spirits of the dead, tombs and statues, the cross and a magic book called the Bible."

CHAPTER 49

Then Aaron let himself be afraid. He let himself think of the one word that on the prairie was as fearful as Fire—Blizzard.

CHAPTER 50

He took her petition for prayer seriously but not for long. He had unhappily noticed at the Mission that when he had most hotly prayed, it had been in a way of escaping a decision, of frivolously passing the lot to God.

CHAPTER 54

In the same week there appeared in St. Paul a German settler who hated all Scandinavians, a Swedish farmer who looked down on all Danes, a Dane who disliked all Norwegians, and a Norwegian pastor who was hoity-toity about all Danes, Swedes, Germans, Irish Catholics, British, Yankees and Jews.

CHAPTER 54

Mrs. Boogus: "I simply cannot abide these ugly, awkward foreign names," said Mrs. Tryphosa Bopp Boogus, who came from Gahgosh Falls.

CHAPTER 54

All of them—well, half of them—unpacked their prejudices before they unpacked their hoes and hymn books. So Aaron watched his world missing a chance that was perhaps unique in history.

Michael Fridgen

World So Wild (1951)

World So Wide was published in 1951, just after Sinclair Lewis passed on to that big Main Street in the sky. It was his only
novel published after his death. Lewis died in Rome and it's
clearly evident that his years living in Italy directly impacted
World So Wide. Although Zenith, Winnemac makes an appearance, most of the book takes place in Florence, Italy.

In many ways, *World So Wide* is a sequel to *Dodsworth*. In
other ways it's a completely new story. Regardless, Sam Dodsworth and Edith Cortright are featured in the novel, and more
than just cameo appearances. Like *Dodsworth*, *World So Wide*
is largely a discussion of the philosophy of traveling abroad.
However, in this work the aspect of travel plays second fiddle
to the main character's romantic interests.

After experiencing a horrific tragedy, Hayden Chart of Colorado seeks to rediscover his life by traveling through Europe.
It seems that Sam Dodsworth and Edith Cortright did not
move back to Zenith and have instead settled in Italy. Hayden
Chart befriends them and their circle of friends. Complicated
romances and their various entanglements ensue.

Don't assume that because *World So Wide* was Sinclair Lewis's only posthumous work it is somehow inferior. The satire
of this book is superior to much of Lewis's later writing. The
character development and romantic plot lines are also better
than in some of his proceeding novels.

Sinclair Lewis was 65 when he died in 1951. Did he have another *Elmer Gantry* in him? Probably not. Lewis was drinking
quite heavily all the way up to his death. He attempted several
times to conquer his alcoholism to no avail. Unfortunately, he
wasn't just a drinker–he suffered from a severe form of the ac-

tual disease of alcoholism. Alcoholism is hard enough to beat today; it was nearly impossible with the limited resources of 1951.

CHAPTER 1
There was something comic in that grotesque horror. The roof was below him, then the car upended like a rearing horse, then his head had struck the roof and afterward the windshield, then the whirling cosmos banged down, and the side window was below him, on the earth, then up beside him again, and they were still. The huge noise dissolved into a huge blank silence, and the car shook like a panting animal.

CHAPTER 3
On the typical Newlife, Colorado belief of the state of European cities: In World War II, some hundreds of local young people had campaigned in Italy and France, and the general city belief was now, and for another ten years probably would be, that all through Europe "conditions" were exactly what they had been in a bombed city in 1944.

CHAPTER 5
Sam Dodsworth: "Don't stay in Italy too long—or anywhere else abroad. It gets you. Since I was fool enough to sell the Revelation Motor Company, Edith and I have drifted through India and China and Austria and God knows where all, and this time, we've been back in Italy for three years—course, Edith's been coming here off and on for many years. Well, we tried to go back and live in the States, in Zenith, but we're kind of spoiled for it. Everybody is so damn busy making money there that you can't find anybody to talk with, unless you're willing to pay for it by busting a gut playing golf.

CHAPTER 6
Dr. Olivia Lomond: "They're all so poor. I hate poor people! I'm so poor myself!

CHAPTER 9

If a queen comes to America, crowds fill the station squares, and attendant British journalists rejoice, "You see: the American Cousins are as respectful to Royalty as we are." But the Americans have read of queens since babyhood. They want to see one queen, once, and if another came to town next week, with twice as handsome a crown, she would not draw more than two small boys and an Anglophile. Americans want to see one movie star, one giraffe, one jet plane, one murder, but only one. They run up a skyscraper or the fame of generals and evangelists and playwrights in one week and tear them all down in an hour, and the mark of excellence everywhere is "under new management."

CHAPTER 9

Once magic touch of Home and he was already back in its good-fellowship, its sterling virtues and its lack of vocabulary.

CHAPTER 9

There is, Hayden found, something like a system of credits for sight-seeing: doing a cathedral thoroughly counts, let us say, eleven points—exterior only, five; looking for not less than one second at every single picture in a large gallery comes to thirteen, inspecting a mountain village rarely beheld by tourists is seventeen, dining at a celebrated restaurant is six, but if you found it all by yourself, the credit is nine. By this most reasonable standard for computing good works, the Windelbanks had acquired at least four times as many points of merit as Hayden.

CHAPTER 14

Then he let them go in to lunch. Lady Belmont was also there, though this is noted, like the day's temperature, only as a matter of record.

CHAPTER 20

Hayden Chart: "It seems natural to be home, where you understand people by instinct, understand why they do the particular things they do do and do say—dumb or dreary or noble and silly."

Conclusion

The word "conclusion" really has no business in any book about the writing of Sinclair Lewis. As I stated near the beginning of this compilation, endings are not something afforded to the readers of realism. We live in a world where people believe that they have an innate right to closure. Unfortunately, as your mom probably told you: life isn't fair.

Sinclair Lewis knew that real life rarely gives closure. It's frustrating as hell for the reader, but the villains in his novels hardly ever get their comeuppance. Neither are the heroes rewarded. The poor often get poorer and people sometimes die for no reason. However, if you spend some time thinking about the lack of closure in Lewis's novels, you'll come away better prepared to face your own life with all its ambiguities and lack of completion.

Perhaps someday someone will make a new film version of *Main Street* or *It Can't Happen Here.* Perhaps that film will trigger a resurgence in the popularity of Sinclair Lewis. But until that time comes, I'll be satisfied to stand atop Inspiration Peak among the Leaf Hills of Minnesota. I'm fortunate to be able see life through Lewis's unique perspective. My fondest wish is that others will also find their fortune within the pages of his books.